BEYOND
the
BERMUDA
TRIANGLE

BEYOND
the
BERMUDA
TRIANGLE

True Encounters With Electronic Fog, Missing Aircraft, and Time Warps

BRUCE GERNON AND ROB MACGREGOR

New Page Books
A Division of The Career Press, Inc.
Wayne, NJ

Beyond the Bermuda Triangle
Edited by Gina Schenck
Typeset by PerfecType, Nashville, Tennessee
Cover design by vril8
Printed in the U.S.A.

To order this title, please call toll-free 1-800-CAREER-1 (NJ and Canada: 201-848-0310) to order using VISA or MasterCard, or for further information on books from Career Press.

The Career Press, Inc.
12 Parish Drive
Wayne, NJ 07470
www.careerpress.com

Library of Congress Cataloging-in-Publication Data

CIP Data Available Upon Request.

DEDICATION

Special thanks to David Pares and Joe McMoneagle for their expertise, and many thanks to all those who contributed stories.

Bruce Gernon
To my beloved wife, Lynn, who has believed in my Bermuda Triangle experience for 44 years, and to my lovely daughter, Keely, who has believed in my experience for 38 years.

Rob MacGregor
To fellow writer and wife, Trish, and fellow writer and daughter, Megan.

ACKNOWLEDGMENTS

We want to thank all of those who have written to us through the years about their extraordinary experiences inside and outside of the Bermuda Triangle. Many of those stories appear in this book.

CONTENTS

INTRODUCTION
DISCOVERING I WASN'T ALONE

I was 23 years old when it happened: the mind-boggling event that changed my life. I'd been flying airplanes with my dad since I was a young teenager and I got my pilot's license when I was 18. Five years later, I was at the controls flying with my dad and his business partner as we departed from Andros Island in the Bahamas. That's when I encountered something strange and frightening, something that literally swallowed our new Bonanza A36 and spit us out a hundred miles from where we'd just been flying.

That was December 4, 1970, and I'd encountered what later became known as the Bermuda Triangle mystery. For months, I puzzled over this seemingly unbelievable sequence of events. I put my story to memory, precisely as I remembered it, and documented the details.

I didn't speak to anyone about it for a little more than a year because I felt like it was impossible to explain exactly what happened. Then I heard there was a mysterious area offshore of Miami where planes and boats were disappearing and I realized what I had flown through must have been the cause of their disappearance. I told everyone I met about it, but at first, it was as if they didn't hear me, except for my dad and our business partner. They always backed up my research.

I was like a tree in the forest that falls and no one hears its thunderous crash. So did it make a sound? Likewise, if teleportation or time travel—or a combination of the two—never happened to anyone else, did this event really occur as I remembered it? What I was saying didn't make sense. It couldn't possibly be true. But I knew what I experienced, and I couldn't stop thinking about it.

After a couple of years, everything changed as I began hearing about the lore of the Bermuda Triangle, the now-legendary zone of mystery outlined by Miami, Bermuda, and Puerto Rico. Through the centuries, thousands of vessels large and small, as well as aircrafts, have vanished in the great expanse. Researchers gathered stories and statistics, and soon articles and books were published.

I discovered that I wasn't alone, that others had encountered this mysterious phenomenon. Their compasses had started spinning, their electronic equipment shut down, and some had leaped through space and time.

People were finally listening to my story and that eventually led to my participation in cable-channel documentaries and my first book, *THE FOG*, coauthored with Rob MacGregor. My story is unique because I flew into the heart of the mystery and lived to tell about it. This is my story. But it's also the story of others who, like me, apparently penetrated a rift in the space-time continuum and found themselves in unexpected places at unexpected times.

Is the Bermuda Triangle a dangerous place? On an average day, hundreds of people fly over it and cruise through it on ships. They don't crash, sink, or disappear. Yet, sometimes it happens, and you never know when the compasses will suddenly start spinning wildly and a fog will surround your craft—a fog that you can't escape. There is no season for the Bermuda Triangle effect. It could happen any time, to anyone.

I recognize that many skeptics and debunkers view the Bermuda Triangle as a non-mystery. They attribute all the missing airplanes and ships to mechanical failures, human error, or bad weather. They reject anything that exceeds known physical laws. Certainly, in some cases, they are correct.

However, to dismiss all that has occurred as a non-mystery shows a lack of willingness to look closely at cases such as mine. As William James once said, "If you wish to upset the law that all crows are black, you mustn't seek to show that no crows are; it is enough if you prove one single crow to be white."

It only takes one white crow to prove that all crows are not black. As I've often said, if any of those researchers had been flying with me on that day in December 1970, they would have a considerably different view on the matter.

Skeptics also point out that similar disappearances involving planes and ships have taken place outside the boundaries of the Bermuda Triangle. In this case, I agree wholeheartedly. In fact, the Bermuda Triangle story is like the final twist in a good mystery in which the vanquished antagonist surprisingly reappears elsewhere, setting up a sequel.

That's exactly the case. Rather than turning into a non-mystery, the phenomenon extends well beyond its triangular boundaries. I've received dozens of stories from people who have encountered what I call "electronic fog," and some of the people have experienced time warps and teleportation. Some of the events occurred in the legendary waters off the east coast of Florida, but others happened elsewhere, including the Pacific Ocean, Lake Michigan, and on land. In essence, there is *no* actual Bermuda Triangle, but places throughout the world where warps in the space-time continuum appear on occasion, sometimes with baffling consequences. From my years of research, I'm convinced these mysterious events that seem outside the realm of possibility could happen virtually anywhere. That includes the Indian Ocean where Malaysian Flight 370 disappeared.

In *Beyond the Bermuda Triangle*, I'll take you first-hand, step-by-step, through my experience. You'll read what I saw, what I felt, and how I reacted. I'll also tell the stories of other pilots and boat captains, as well as the tales of people who have encountered the fog while walking at night on a golf course or driving their cars in remote areas. I'll include stories from famed pilot Charles Lindbergh and aeronautical author Martin Caidin, and even Christopher Columbus.

I'll take you to meet physics professor David Pares, a former Army meteorologist, who believes my experience holds an important key to creating a warp drive that can take us to the stars. Amazingly, Pares is building such a ship in his garage!

I know that some readers will find these stories hard to believe. That's especially true when we enter the realm of UFOs and their possible involvement in breaches of the space-time continuum. I can't prove what happened to other people whose stories I've included, but I know what happened to me.

In my case, I was stunned by the behavior of an enormous cloud that seemed to be chasing me, that seemed to be sentient, conscious, by the fog that surrounded the plane mile after mile, by the malfunctioning of all my electronic equipment, including two compasses. When we contacted Miami radio, the tower informed us that the weather between Bimini and Miami was clear and there was no plane on the radar. What? How could that be?

Then things got even stranger and more disturbing. I'll explain it all in detail in the first chapter. I know this story because I've been thinking about it almost every day since it happened.

Chapter
1

The Journey

The Island

It's the largest and least-populated island in the Bahamas; larger than all the others put together. There's a mystique about the place, an island with its own mythology. Yet Andros Island is not as widely known or visited as the tourist destinations of Nassau and Freeport. It's mostly forested with hundreds of tiny islets and 178 blue holes—entrances to a vast underwater cave system that pockets the island.

I'll talk more about the island in Chapter 9, but I wanted to mention Andros right away because it's where my flight began, the one that changed my life and opened a window that I've never been able to close.

The reason I was on the island on Dec. 4, 1970, was because my father and a business partner, Chuck Layfayette, were scouting Andros as a potential location to build a resort. We had already flown here from West Palm Beach more than a dozen times and I was very familiar with the route from Andros to Bimini, to Miami Beach, then along the coast to West Palm.

Although my father was also a pilot, I was at the controls of our new Bonanza A36 that day. In fact, I had become the regular pilot on these flights. The Bonanza A36 is a stable, smooth-flying craft, and even today the Bonanza airframe remains relatively unchanged and is one of general aviation's finest performing airplanes. That was fortunate for us, because if we had left the island on a slower, less stable plane, I'm not sure we would've survived.

We had planned to take off that morning, but it was raining, so we waited until the weather improved. I've always been a cautious pilot, and even at 23 years old I wasn't a dare-devil or thrill-seeker. It was close to 3 p.m. when we were ready to take off from Andros Town Airport.

I remember that the sky was overcast and a light mist was falling. Weather information wasn't available, so I decided to get airborne, then call Miami Flight Service for atmospheric conditions. After taking off, I made a turn and looked over to the terminal, where I saw my friend, John Woolbright, waving to me. John was a mathematician at the Atlantic Undersea Test Evaluation Center (AUTEC), a U.S. Navy facility based on the island. Ironically, AUTEC would play a role in the Bermuda Triangle saga. Keep in mind, however, that at the time I didn't know anything about the mystery, and had never heard the term "Bermuda Triangle."

Mystery Cloud

We climbed to 1,000 feet and assumed a compass heading of 315 degrees, which is northwest. We couldn't go any higher because of a cloud ceiling at 1,500 feet. My father was an expert navigator, as well as a pilot, so we flew the plane together on a direct route to Bimini. We tuned into the Bimini radio beacon on our automatic direction finder, and also used a magnetic compass.

We were cruising at 180 miles an hour and had been flying for about 10 minutes when the drizzle ended and the skies cleared. By then, we had reached the northwest end of Andros Island and were flying over the ocean shallows of the Great Bahama Bank. The visibility had improved from about three miles to 10 miles and the weather ahead appeared non-threatening.

As we started to gain altitude, I noticed an oval-shaped cloud directly in front of us, about two miles away. From its appearance, I assumed it was a lenticular cloud. While other clouds move across the sky with the air currents, lenticular clouds tend to remain stationary. The cloud appeared to be about a mile-and-a-half long and a thousand feet thick, with the top of it reaching an altitude of 1,500 feet.

It was white, with smooth edges, and appeared inoffensive. However, there was something unusual about it. I'd seen quite a few lenticular clouds, but never at such a low altitude. They usually are seen at high altitudes, 20,000 to 40,000 feet.

We passed over the cloud, but I couldn't spend much time looking at it because I was intent on filing my flight plan with Miami Flight Service. Miami Radio, the call sign for the flight service, offered a promising forecast. The weather would be clear between Andros and the Florida coast, with a few scattered, isolated thunderstorms of moderate intensity in South Florida. Winds were light and variable and the temperature was 75 degrees.

We were about 10 miles offshore and climbing toward our intended altitude of 10,500 feet when I noticed that the cloud we had passed was no longer a stationary lenticular cloud—if it ever was one. It had shifted into a huge, billowy, white, cumulus-shaped cloud. We were climbing at a thousand feet per minute, and the cloud seemed to be building up underneath us at the same rate that we were ascending.

It rose so quickly that it occurred to me that we were flying above a cumulonimbus cloud, one of the most dangerous clouds for a pilot to encounter, and that it was about to form a monstrous thunderhead. Chuck, who was seated in the rear, started to get nervous. He had never come this close to a cloud while flying in a small plane. I assured him that we would break free of it at any moment.

After all, we were flying at more than 100 miles an hour as we ascended, and how fast could a cloud move? The answer depends on the kind of cloud and its location. Wispy cirrus clouds can move in excess of 100 miles an hour in the jet stream at about 20,000 feet— more than three miles high. However, clouds associated with thunderstorms, like the one following us, can only travel at 30 to 40 miles an hour. So how could this cloud keep pace with us?

Several minutes passed as we continued our ascent. We had reached nearly a mile high, but somehow that cloud was still climbing with us, as if it was actually chasing us. To my surprise, the cloud caught us and engulfed the plane. How was this possible? We felt a slight updraft and visibility shrank to less than a hundred feet. After about 30 seconds, we broke free and continued our ascent.

But the cloud was still right below us, rising with us. I couldn't even get 10 yards above the cloud and, after another half-minute, it closed around us again. Suddenly, another updraft gave us an unexpected burst of acceleration that pushed us above the cloud. But after several seconds our vertical speed diminished and the cloud caught up to us again. The scenario was repeated at least five more times. Dad and Chuck were getting worried, and Dad suggested we return to Andros.

However, making a 180-degree turn would be risky. That might take us right into the storm. I was considering it when we suddenly burst free of the cloud at 11,500 feet. I leveled the Bonanza and accelerated to a cruising speed of 195 miles per hour. What I didn't realize at the time was that the cloud must have been moving horizontally at a speed of at least 105 miles an hour, as well as rising vertically. But when it stopped its horizontal movement, we escaped it.

When I looked back, I was astonished at what I saw. The small saucer-shaped cloud that we had flown over had metastasized into an immense squall. But unlike most squalls, which form a line, this cloud curved in a perfect semicircle and radiated out on either side of us. It appeared to extend at least 10 miles on our right and the same distance on the left.

After a few minutes, we left the cloud behind and continued under clear skies toward Bimini. I engaged the auto-pilot, sat back, and started to relax. Everything was back to normal, or so I thought. I didn't realize that the challenge was just beginning and we hadn't escaped at all.

Lindy's Lost Flight

Before I continue with my story, I want to tell you about another flight through the Bermuda Triangle by one of the most celebrated pilots of all time. Charles Lindbergh became famous for making the first solo transatlantic flight in his plane, *Spirit of St. Louis*, on May 20–21, 1927. He was 25 years old and had only been flying for four years when he made the flight from New York to Paris.

However, in spite of his celebrity status—or maybe because of it— Lindbergh remained silent about a flight he made nine months later when he encountered conditions that puzzled him for the rest of his life. The story finally became known four years after his death, when his autobiography was published in 1978.

Lindbergh took off at 1:35 a.m. on Feb. 13, 1928, on the last leg of an around-the-Gulf-and-Caribbean tour. He would fly from Havana to St. Louis in what, for him, should have been a long, but routine flight. It would also be the first-ever direct flight between the two cities. "It should've been an easy flight—about a third the distance from New York to Paris," he wrote in his 1978 book, *Autobiography of Values.* However, that's not what happened.

He climbed to an altitude of 4,000 feet and settled back to enjoy the night flight. "But halfway across the Straits of Florida my magnetic compass started rotating, and the earth–inductor-compass needle jumped back and forth erratically. By that time, a haze had formed, screening off horizons."

Only one other time had he seen two compasses fail simultaneously. That was during a storm in the Atlantic en route to Paris, and his magnetic compass only oscillated back and forth, so he was able to calculate his direction by the central point of the oscillation. But this time the magnetic compass spun in circles and the inductor compass was useless. "I had no idea whether I was flying north, south, east, or west."

Lindbergh started climbing toward the clear sky that just minutes before had been above him. If he could find Polaris, he could navigate by the stars. But the haze thickened as he gained altitude. So he descended to less than a thousand feet, but the haze followed him and he could barely see the ocean.

Just before dawn, he spotted a shadowy island and assumed that he'd reached the Florida Keys. But after crossing a narrow body of water, Lindbergh saw a long coastline bending to the right, the opposite way that the land curved on his map of Florida. "But if I was not flying over a Florida key, where could I be? Was it possible I had returned to Cuba, that my attempt to read the twirling compasses had put me one-hundred-eighty degrees off course?"

The coastline ended and he saw more keys ahead. He realized that if he wasn't over the Florida Keys, he was over the Bahamas. That meant he had been flying at a 90-degree angle from his proper heading and that he was about 300 miles off course. Once the sun was high enough above the horizon, he determined east and headed through the haze in the opposite direction, toward the Florida coast. The magnetic compass stopped rotating as soon as he reached the mainland. He passed by dozens of heavy squalls as he moved through Florida and Georgia, and headed on to St. Louis to complete his flight.

Lindbergh never talked publicly about his strange experience in what was to become known as the Bermuda Triangle. No doubt he survived the experience because of his incredible abilities as a pilot.

That flight would be merely an interesting footnote to his flying career and celebrated life, and nothing more, were it not for the fact that he documented a case of an aeronautical encounter with a rare but often deadly phenomenon that remains a scientific anomaly.

Forty-two years later, I encountered a similar fog. In some respects, my flight was even more harrowing than Lindbergh's. But I'm getting ahead of myself.

Surrounded

After a few minutes of flying under clear skies and moving closer and closer to Bimini, we noticed a squall forming in front of us. As we approached the cloud, moving at about three miles a minute, an eerie sight unfolded. To my consternation, the cloud looked very much like the one we had left behind. It had a similar curving, semi-circular shape, except the arms extended in the opposite direction, as if attempting to embrace us. The cloud was enormous, its top reaching at least 40,000 feet.

Then I noticed something else that stunned me: Normal cumulus clouds have a base or ceiling, 1,000 to 2,000 feet above the surface. If the cloud is producing rain, the base is usually at about 1,000 feet and sometimes as low as 400 or 500 hundred feet. But, as we flew within a few miles of the cloud, I saw that this cloud appeared to emanate directly from the ocean.

I realized that we couldn't go under the cloud or above it, and attempting to circumvent it would take us considerably off our flight path. Besides, the arms of the cloud were already stretching out on either side of us, so we couldn't make an easy escape. However, the cloud didn't look too threatening, so after conferring with Dad, I decided to fly into it.

I had flown under clouds in heavy rain and I had penetrated them while flying with instrument-rated pilots. But pilots are supposed to steer clear of strong thunderstorms, and the 10,000-foot level was supposed to be the most dangerous altitude to fly through a storm. I had been told that there could be updrafts and downdrafts in excess of 100 miles an hour in the heart of a thunderstorm cell.

We were about 45 miles east of Bimini when we entered the misty edges of this enormous cloud formation. Once inside, I realized I might have made a mistake. Although the cloud was white and fluffy on the outside, the interior was dark, as if night suddenly had fallen. But it didn't stay dark for long. Bright white flashes lit up the interior of the cloud. They seemed to go on and off in a never-ending, random pattern, and the deeper we penetrated, the more intense the flashes became.

Even though there were no bolts of lightning, I had no doubt that we had entered an electrical storm. We were in trouble and I was getting more concerned by the second. When my father asked if I was going to continue on, I shook my head. I immediately turned 135 degrees and assumed a due south heading.

We were all wearing watches and noted that we were deviating from our course at 3:27 p.m. An electric-powered clock on the panel, which included a timer that I had engaged upon takeoff, indicated that we had been airborne for 27 minutes. When we changed course, my father started the timer on his watch, and by using the plane's navigational equipment, he calculated that we were 40 miles southeast of Bimini. Meanwhile, I contacted Miami Radio and told them that we had altered our course to avoid a thunderstorm and were attempting to fly around it.

We were still concerned about our situation, but we thought we might be able to avoid the semicircular-shaped cloud to the south by flying around it. However, after traveling six or seven miles we could see that the cloud continued on our left to the east. A couple minutes later, we realized we were in serious trouble. Astonishingly, the cloud that we had encountered near Andros was now connected with the second storm cloud. As far as I could tell, the enormous cloud encircled us. I estimated that the diameter of the opening was about 30 miles. We were trapped inside a huge donut hole, a billowing prison with no way out. We couldn't fly over it. We couldn't fly under it.

A Perilous Escape

Now I was really getting worried, but I knew I needed to remain calm. When I tried to understand how we had gotten into this predicament, a stray thought came to mind: I remembered my mother telling me numerous times as I grew up that I had been born during the largest, most powerful thunderstorm that she had ever witnessed. Now here I was inside what might be the last thunderstorm I would ever encounter.

It seemed that the storm was created initially from a saucer-shaped cloud just offshore of Andros Island. It had rapidly spread outward, forming the donut hole, when it connected with a similar cloud. I recalled what it was like inside the thunderstorm, and I definitely didn't want to fly back into the powerful storm cell.

We had flown about 10 miles from the point where we turned south when I noticed an opening in the massive cloud. At the top of the cloud, on either side, the arms extended outward above the opening. It looked as if the arms would soon connect, creating a bridge and forming a tunnel. The anvil shape is commonly seen in cumulonimbus thunderstorms as they reach maturity. The top typically spreads outward for several miles at 35,000 feet. Normally, I would stay clear of any anvil-shaped clouds, but our situation required drastic action.

Faced with the dilemma we were in, I felt that I had no choice but to turn the aircraft 90 degrees to the right and try to exit through the cloud by way of the only visible opening. As we flew toward the aperture, we saw the two anvil heads connect, forming a tunnel that was about a mile wide and appeared to be between 10 and 15 miles long.

Its center was at our altitude of 10,000 feet. On the far side of the passage, we could see blue sky. That gave us hope.

As we neared the tunnel, we realized that its diameter was shrinking. So I took the engine up to maximum power. By the time we were three miles away, the opening was only about a thousand feet wide. I recalled what my first flight instructor, Charles Galanza, told us in class one night: Sometimes in the higher altitudes, usually above 5,000 feet, long horizontal tunnels sometimes formed in storm clouds. He called them "sucker holes," and warned us never to fly through them. He said he knew of pilots who had tried the feat and were never seen again. I assumed he meant that they had crashed into the ocean and disappeared.

We were still two miles away when the opening shrank to 500 feet. But there was no turning back. We were committed. As we approached the opening, the aperture was about 300 feet wide and still shrinking.

Gernon enters the tunnel vortex. Photo credit: Bruce Gernon.

The Tunnel and Beyond

As soon as we flew into the tunnel, I was startled by strange spiraling lines embedded on the interior of the tunnel walls. They looked like puffs of gray clouds about three feet long and a foot thick that swirled around the plane in a counterclockwise motion. Moments before the tunnel had appeared to be 10 miles long. Now it appeared to be about a mile long and we could still see blue sky on the other side. Instead of three minutes, it would only take us only 20 seconds to pass through the tunnel. I tried to remain right in the center of the opening. I was afraid that if the wings brushed the edges of the cloud I might lose sight of the hole and the path to the clear sky.

The silky white walls of the tunnel glowed with the light from the afternoon sun, and the tunnel was still shrinking. The diameter of the tunnel was only 30 feet and the tips of the wings scraped the edges of the cloud as we reached the far side and escaped the collapsing tunnel.

That's when I suddenly felt weightless and knew my seatbelt was the only thing keeping me from rising out of my seat. It was the only time I've ever experienced the sensation in my 50 years of flying. It felt like zero gravity, but it also felt like I was hydroplaning. At the same time, I noticed vapor at the ends of the wings that created parallel trails behind us. It also felt as if the plane was increasing in speed. After about 10 seconds, the weightless sensation vanished.

I looked back and gasped as I watched the tunnel walls form a slowly rotating slit. I was relieved that we made it through, but I felt disoriented and asked my dad to check our position. He was always good at using the instruments to give me our exact location on the chart.

This time he fiddled with the instruments for longer than usual. Then he said something was wrong. That was when I realized that all the electronic and magnetic navigational instruments were malfunctioning. Even the magnetic compass was slowly rotating counterclockwise, as if the plane were making a turn.

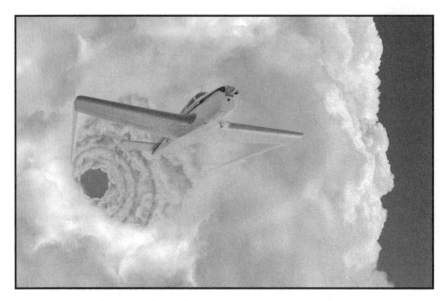

Gernon exits the tunnel as electronic fog captures his plane.
Photo credit: Bruce Gernon.

Now, instead of the clear blue sky, everything appeared a dull grayish white. Visibility appeared to be more than two miles, but there was absolutely nothing to see—no ocean, no sky, no horizon, only a gray haze. Although haze in the lower atmosphere is common, this haze was darker than normal. But the air was stable and there was no lightning or precipitation. We seemed to be in some sort of fog, but unlike the usual fog where visibility is never much more than a few hundred feet, we could see much farther. Even more disturbing was the fact that the instruments continued malfunctioning.

I contacted Miami air-traffic control and reported that I wasn't sure of our position and would like radar identification. The plane was equipped with a transponder, a new invention in 1970 that helped radar controllers identify the location of airplanes. I told them that we were about 45 miles southeast of Bimini heading east and flying at 10,000 feet. But the controller came back and said there were no planes on radar between Miami, Bimini, and Andros. That was when

Dad snatched the microphone and yelled at the controller. "What the hell do you mean you can't find us on radar?"

It was a terrifying moment. We literally didn't exist, at least not on radar. Had we crashed and died, and didn't know it? I didn't think so. But it was probably fortunate that I didn't know anything about the Bermuda Triangle—none of the bizarre stories—because I was inside of one!

The controller sounded bewildered and apologized, but said the radar showed no blips in the area where we were flying. I wondered how that could be. In the past, they had always been able to identify us, especially when we were approaching the air defense identification zone (ADIZ).

Dad was getting more and more agitated and began screaming at the controller. He was starting to panic so I took the microphone back and told the controller to let us know if anything came up on his radar. Meanwhile, Chuck looked woozy, as if he might pass out. Later, he would tell his children that the hands on his watch were spinning as we passed through the tunnel, but I think it only appeared that way to him because of his state of mind. I did my best to calm Dad and Chuck by saying that we were through the worst of it. Everything else would be okay.

But I was wrong. It was about to get much more baffling and disturbing.

Dislocation

I slowed the plane down to a maneuvering speed of 180 miles per hour, because I didn't know what would happen next. I remembered that when we entered the tunnel our heading was 290 degrees, but now the compass was spinning. Very soon we could be going in any direction, including right back into the dangerous cloud. Desperation and anxiety crawled across the pit of my stomach. I focused on creating an imaginary compass in my mind that was pointed to true north. I'd experimented with this idea before with some positive results. I set the imaginary compass to a 290-degree heading.

At this point, we had been traveling for nearly 32 minutes. According to our flight time, we should have been approaching the chain of Bimini islands, which extend 55 miles south of Bimini, the main island, to Orange Cay, the southernmost island in the chain. I estimated that we were about 95 miles southwest of Miami, and just shy of 20 miles from crossing the Bimini chain. If my internal compass was working, I figured we would be crossing the islands in six or seven minutes. If it wasn't working, well, we wouldn't be heading anywhere near Miami. That was for certain.

Off to the right, we saw a dark area that looked like land. But it was too soon for the islands. I figured it was probably the shadow of a cloud rather than an island. Pilots often mistake such shadows for islands when flying in the Bahamas, especially when they're getting anxious to find a checkpoint. As we flew past the dark spot, it seemed to pass by us much too quickly. So I decided it must be the shadow of a dingy dark cloud moving in the opposite direction.

We continued on, still shrouded by the odd haze. I was puzzled by the conditions, but the air remained stable and I felt in control of the airplane. We were still on the Miami frequency, but hadn't heard any transmissions for several minutes. That seemed odd. Then, suddenly, the controller yelled out that he had spotted an airplane directly over Miami Beach, flying due west.

I looked at my watch and saw that we had been flying for just under 34 minutes. We couldn't possibly be over Miami Beach already, so I told the controller that we were approximately 90 miles southwest of Miami, and still looking for the Bimini chain of islands.

Suddenly, the fog started to break apart, but it didn't just dissipate. Long ribbons of fog ran parallel along our direction of flight. The ribbons appeared to spread apart about one mile from the plane, and ran two to three miles in front of us, and about the same distance behind us. The slits gradually grew wider and then within several seconds, the ribbons of fog disappeared. I call it "electronic dissipation."

All I could see was brilliant blue sky. As our eyes adjusted to the brightness, we were astonished to see Miami Beach directly below us. We were relieved to see familiar land again and to have escaped the fog. But how did we get here? I knew it was important to remember the cloud and the fog, to remember everything that had happened. It was an odd thought, almost as if it had come from outside of me. The cloud we had gone through was certainly extraordinary, but I had no idea how or why it would be significant.

The fog breaks up as Gernon and his two passengers arrive unexpectedly in Miami Beach. Photo credit: Bruce Gernon.

Survivors (from left) Bruce Gernon, Chuck Layfayette, Bruce Gernon Sr., 25 years after their flight through the Bermuda Triangle phenomenon. Photo credit: Lynn Gernon.

Dad noticed that the navigation instruments appeared to be working again, so he used them to verify our position. I contacted the radar controller and told him that he was correct about our location over Miami Beach. I thanked him for his assistance and signed off the radio.

We headed north and skirted around a thunderstorm near Fort Lauderdale. After we landed at Palm Beach International, I was puzzled that the flight had taken 47 minutes. I thought something must be wrong with the plane's timer. But all three of our watches showed that it was 3:48 p.m. The airplane clock showed the same time.

I had made the flight from Palm Beach to Andros at least a dozen times and had never flown it in less than 75 minutes, and that was on a direct route. This flight was indirect and probably covered a distance of close to 250 miles. The Bonanza could not possibly travel that distance in 47 minutes when its maximum cruising speed was 195 miles an hour. We had no answers. We had arrived nearly half an hour too early, and I would find out that we had 10 gallons of extra fuel that should have been burned off. I still have the gas receipts to prove it!

Another year would pass before I realized that our experience was part of a larger story. We had encountered and survived what was becoming known as the Bermuda Triangle.

Bruce Gernon in his hangar.
Photo credit: Lynn Gernon.

chapter 2

Bermuda Past

I've received hundreds of e-mails throughout the years from people who have seen me recount my experience on documentaries or read *THE FOG*. Some of the correspondents included their own stories, or second-hand stories. For example, Marilyn wrote to tell me how, as a child, she heard about a ship that disappeared from Philadelphia, reappeared in Norfolk where she lived, then vanished and reappeared back in Philadelphia. In 1956 or 1957, when she heard this story from a young friend, she doubted the girl, who adamantly defended the story and said her father saw it happen. Decades later, Marilyn was shocked when a movie called *The Philadelphia Experiment* came out and portrayed the same event.

That's hearsay. Marilyn wasn't there. But I also received first-hand stories, and some are startling. Among them is one that involves romance, time travel, and possibly a past-life encounter. It seemed so incredible that my coauthor, Rob MacGregor, began researching the story, analyzing details against historical fact, and exchanging numerous e-mails with both parties involved. He considers it one of the most convincing accounts of time travel ever recorded.

John and Barbara

In 1964, John Murphy was stationed aboard a U.S. Coast Guard cutter that was docked at Pennos Wharf near St. George, Bermuda, on Thanksgiving Day. John went ashore in the afternoon after a Thanksgiving dinner with three of his friends and the four men happened to meet four student nurses in the U.S. Navy Nurse Corps. It was a nice coincidence that would become a very meaningful one for John Murphy. The nursing students had caught a "hop" on an Air Force cargo flight from Wisconsin and were staying in a hotel in St. George.

John was instantly attracted to one of the young women and she seemed equally interested in him. After taking the nurses on a tour of the ship, they debarked as four couples. John and his new friend, Barbara, went off on their own toward Fort St. Catherine, a British fortress with roots dating back to 1612. It was rebuilt several times through the centuries. They sat on a wall near the fort and watched the sunset. They both confessed that they had an overwhelming and uncanny sense that they already knew each other. Yet, both were engaged to someone back in the States and neither one was looking to have an affair.

As the sun sank into the sea, they abandoned the wall and felt drawn toward a narrow lane heading away from the fort. It was barely light when they came upon a small rise in the road and found themselves captured by a sense of eeriness again. They each seemed to know what was on the other side of the hill, even though neither had ever come this way. John said they would see a small 18th-century British village with a church dominating the village square. Barbara had a similar reaction and added that they would see a clock on the steeple of the church. It was broken and displayed the time of 12:30.

When they reached the crest of the hill, they were amazed and startled to see everything as they envisioned it, including the clock stuck at 12:30. As they walked downhill toward the village, they both felt a sense of familiarity. They didn't see any people, but most of the structures were illuminated by lanterns visible inside their windows.

As they walked past the church, they felt drawn to the large graveyard beside it. Holding each other's hands with only a flashlight for illumination, they walked through the cemetery and then sat down on a low stone wall separating the two major sections of the graveyard—one side for whites, the other for blacks. They somehow knew the graveyard's segregated layout.

Nothing about that evening seemed normal. John recalls a strong sense that he not only had visited the village before, but that it had been their home in the past. As they talked, John says they recalled their lives as a married couple with children, and that they had somehow met their deaths together very nearby. They felt a chill and knew there had been something unusual about their deaths.

Barbara spread out a blanket she had in her bag from when she and her friends had gone to the beach earlier in the day. They laid down and John felt an overwhelming sense of love and passion. They held each other close and then, rather than engaging in furtive graveyard sex, something unexpected happened. John recalls: "I closed my eyes and leaned forward to kiss her, but before our lips came together, everything around us grew dark and it felt as if we were tumbling together into a bottomless abyss. The sensation of falling finally ended and then, without any warning...both of us passed out."

They awakened a couple of hours later feeling confused, and quickly left the village. They returned to the hotel in St. George where Barbara and her friends were staying. They awkwardly said their goodbyes, exchanged addresses, and went their separate ways. She would fly back to the States the next day and he would remain in Bermuda for 10 more days.

The Second Look

John had a vivid dream that night about the village and when he woke up, he knew he had to go back and find out more about its history. A couple of days later he was given shore leave and he immediately headed for the village. He wanted to see if he would feel the same sense of eeriness that he had felt there with Barbara. But he also wanted to re-create that sense of being with her and the uncanny feeling that they had lived there as husband and wife.

When he reached the top of the rise, he paused and was dumbfounded by what he saw. There was no sign of a village, just open pastureland. John had arrived without the slightest inklings that he would find no trace of the village. "I fully expected it to be there. In addition to wanting to see it in the daytime, I was going to find a place to sit and write a letter to Barbara. I was totally surprised and found it hard to believe when it wasn't there."

He later added: "I don't know if it's important, but thought you might want to know that we were able to touch and feel the houses and the church and both of us sat on the graveyard wall. These were solid objects and not projections or holographic images. Also, when we tried to enter the church, the doors wouldn't open, but they definitely made noise when I pulled and pushed on the door handle. So there were definitely sounds."

After making sure he was in the right place, he gave up and started back to the ship. However, on the way he stopped at a pub in St. George for a couple of drinks to settle his nerves. An elderly man was tending bar and John asked him if he knew anything about an old neighboring village. The bartender said he had heard of a hamlet in the direction that John had pointed. It existed in the 1700s, but was wiped out by the "great hurricane" in the late 18th century.

That hurricane is known variously as the Great Hurricane of 1780, Hurricane San Calixto, the Great Hurricane of the Antilles, and the 1780 Disaster. The massive storm roared through the Lesser Antilles,

Puerto Rico, Hispaniola, and Bermuda in mid-October of that year. Between 20,000 and 22,000 people were killed. Winds gusted up to 200 miles an hour and it is considered the deadliest hurricane ever to hit the Atlantic.

John thanked the man and as he reached the door, the bartender suggested that he visit an old sea captain in St. George named Sam. He said that he thought the captain's ancestors used to live in the lost village and that it was called St. Catherine. He then sketched a map on a napkin showing John where the captain lived. But then he remembered that he had heard through the island "grape vine" that Sam was away on an extended trip to England and wouldn't return until the first of the year.

John decided to see for himself and easily found the house. A neighbor leaned out a window and said the captain wouldn't be back for several weeks. Disappointed, he walked to the town square and joined some of his friends at the White Horse Tavern. Two of his shipmates, who had been with Barbara's friends, bragged about how they made out with the student nurses. Before anyone asked him about his time with Barbara, he finished his drink and returned to the ship. He was sure he would be coming back to Bermuda sometime within the next year, and he would have another chance to find the captain.

A Clue From the Past

Two days later, John got early liberty approved and went into town on a research mission. He wanted to see if he could find out anything about the sleepy hamlet that he still wasn't completely certain had ever existed. His first stop was at the modest two-room cultural center in St. George. He walked through all the displays of memorabilia from St. George's long history. He paged through photo albums and scrapbooks, hoping to find something that would reference the mysterious village.

He eventually found an item that caught his attention: One of the photo albums included a picture of a man wearing a nautical hat, who stood by several paintings. The caption identified him as Captain Sam, the man John wanted to find. The portrait to his right featured a man and a woman he assumed to be members of his family. What startled John was the image of the woman—she looked so much like Barbara that the two women could have passed for twins. He decided right then that he definitely needed to meet Captain Sam the next time he was in port.

A Mystery at Sea

The next day, John went out to sea on his ship, the cutter *Half Moon*, where the crew practiced ditch-and-rescue landing protocols that prepared the crew for real-life rescues of ditched aircrafts. The drills kept him occupied so he didn't think about St. Catherine and Barbara for a while. Later, during similar night exercises, John was on the 8-to-12 watch when he and other crew members began seeing a large land mass on the radar where no island existed. The only land within range was Bermuda and that was off the other side of the ship. Whatever they were seeing was something else.

When the electronic technicians checked out the radar, they were unable to find anything wrong. The chief technician turned on the air-search radar just to see if the land mass showed up on it as well. As soon as the set warmed up, they saw the same clearly defined outline, like a small island with no bays. It looked to be about three miles in diameter and was at least 10 miles from the ship.

Up on the bridge, the quartermaster on watch laughed and asked if they had found Atlantis or some other mystical place. After all that had happened to John during the previous few days, nothing would have surprised him. A few minutes before 11, the strange land mass echoes suddenly vanished. On one sweep of the antenna they were plainly visible. On the next they were gone. John couldn't help but wonder why things kept appearing and disappearing here on the edge of the Bermuda Triangle.

Aftermath

John had one final opportunity to go ashore before the *Half Moon* departed from Bermuda. After a stop at the White Horse Tavern, he walked alone out to St. Catherine's beach. He closed his eyes and pictured the beautiful enchanting young woman he had met a few days earlier. He already missed her and had the terrible fear that he would never see her again. Finally, he turned back to St. George and slowly walked back to the ship feeling lonely and depressed.

Two days later, the ship departed for New York. The Bermuda trip had been more eventful than he could have imagined. But now, as Bermuda receded into the distance, John needed to sort out his feelings about Barbara and his fiancée. By the time they docked three days later, he had decided to put his memories of Barbara aside and concentrate on his relationship with the girl he planned to marry. However, it didn't work out that way. The reunion was bittersweet, fraught with tension and disappointment. A couple of months later, he broke off the engagement.

Meanwhile, John and Barbara exchanged a series of letters. His feelings for her undoubtedly contributed to his decision in February to end his engagement. He tried to express how he felt in his letters, but found it difficult to explain his sentiments. He wrote several poems that he was certain did an infinitely better job.

Barbara initially was receptive to his amorous entreaties via mail, yet wasn't able to match the degree of his affection. She was still involved with another man who wanted to marry her, but John sensed there was something missing in the relationship. He described her letters as sweet and affectionate, and especially appreciative of his romantic poetry.

While he was courting her through the mail, he never mentioned what happened when he went back to the village. He explained that he didn't know anything about the village. "I didn't want her to think I was some kind of a nut by telling her the place was gone or had been an illusion until I had some explanation." But in April, he would return to Bermuda with the intent of verifying that the village had existed and learning anything else he could about it.

Back to Bermuda

As part of the Coast Guard's oceanography school, John's class took a training cruise that started in Portland, Maine, and ended in St. George, Bermuda. When they arrived at the island, he received a full day of liberty. As soon as he could get away from his shipmates, he went to look for Captain Sam. This time he found him at home.

After knocking on his door, John introduced himself to the stooped elderly man with thinning gray hair and explained the reason for his visit. He told Captain Sam that he felt he had some connection with the lost village of St. Catherine and that he had heard Sam would know about it. The captain seemed puzzled and somewhat wary until John explained he was a sailor from the U.S. Coast Guard cutter *Half Moon*. Sam nodded and welcomed John into his home.

John told him that he had seen the photograph of Sam standing alongside a painting of a couple, and how the woman in the picture looked a lot like an American woman he had met in Bermuda. Sam led him into his parlor and showed him the portrait that was in the photograph. The man was dressed in a naval uniform and the young woman was wearing what appeared to be a gold-colored gown. The captain explained that they were his great-great grandparents and this was their wedding portrait. It was painted by a renowned English artist of the time. They were married in 1764, and they died in 1780 in the great hurricane that destroyed the village.

The young woman in the painting had an uncanny resemblance to Barbara and he wished he had a photo of her. The captain looked him over and said he could see a certain resemblance between John and the naval officer. John didn't think the similarity was very strong, not compared to Barbara and her counterpart. Out of curiosity, he asked the captain for their names. When he heard the answer, John was so stunned he had to sit down: Their names were Sir John and Lady Barbara.

He looked up at the old man's craggy weathered face and told him that was his own name and his friend's name, and that they had walked into the village last November. Captain Sam squinted at him, then sat down in the chair next to him. He asked John to explain what he meant, and John told him all he remembered. By the time he finished, he was wondering if Sam thought he was a lunatic.

Sam reached into a dusty old cabinet next to the table and took out a stack of paper, paged through them, and began telling him about Sir John and Lady Barbara. He explained that the young woman was of noble birth, while her husband was the naval attaché to the governor of the British colony. He had been knighted by King George for several acts of heroism, including one in the Philippine Islands in which he was injured. He was then posted to Bermuda where he met Barbara.

Captain Sam went on to say that Barbara was in the final weeks of pregnancy when the deadly hurricane struck Bermuda. Her body was found the next morning on a hill when the water receded. A midwife cut her open and removed the baby who amazing was still alive. The baby survived and ultimately became the captain's great-grandfather.

"Dear John"

Two days later, John was at the campus in Connecticut after he and fellow students took a flight back. Now he couldn't wait to tell Barbara what he had learned. Unfortunately, there was a "Dear John" letter waiting for him. Barbara asked him not to write her anymore. She wanted to focus on her relationship with her fiancé.

Talk about bad timing. That was the first time John ever went out and got "rip-roaring" drunk.

~~~~~

I found this story fascinating. Did John really find his own great-great-grandson from another life that he and Barbara lived? John believes so. Likewise, he is convinced that he and Barbara traveled through the veil of time to the lost village of St. Catherine. I'm well aware that John's story isn't proof of either time travel or past lives. Like my own story, it's anecdotal evidence, which to mainstream science is equivalent to no evidence. Yet, I know what happened to me, and John attests the same about his experience.

But I knew John's story would take on more reality if Barbara confirmed it. I wanted to know if he ever saw her again. Did he ever have the chance to tell her the village had vanished? And what did she remember?

As the years went by, John continued to be haunted by this incident. In 2008, he happened to see a documentary about Bermuda, which led him to begin searching for the student nurse he had met decades earlier. Was she still alive? Would she even remember meeting him? His search took months because he didn't know her last name, or even the correct spelling of her maiden name, or where she lived. While hunting for any traces of Barbara, he found her engagement announcement in a Wisconsin newspaper. It was dated April 14, 1965, which was near the time he had received the Dear John letter that ended their long-distance relationship.

That led him to wonder what would have happened if he had reached Barbara with his newfound information before she committed to the engagement. "Who knows what might've unfolded under those circumstances. It might've made a difference in both of our current lives."

John continued his search and followed a trail from her high school yearbook to a nursing pamphlet to a nursing registry, and finally found her address and phone number. He was nervous when he called her, not knowing if she would remember him or that night so long ago in Bermuda. He left a message and anxiously awaited a return call.

Finally, hours later, she called. She remembered him, and she remembered the village. At last, after four decades, he told her what happened when he went back, and told her about Captain Sam and the history of the village.

Because this story is so astonishing, we wanted to confirm it with Barbara for ourselves. John provided Rob with her email address and he wrote her. How much did she remember? Did she believe that she lived in that village in a past life? She replied the next day. Yes, she definitely recalled the village, as John had said, and she also remembers they both fell asleep near the graveyard. However, she doesn't remember all the details, including the clock stuck at 12:30. Although she remembers feeling attracted to the village, she didn't think in terms of it being a past-life residence. She recalls:

> Fifty-two years ago, I was 19 years old and had no awareness of "past lives." When I met John, he was respectful, comforting and safe to be with so it felt okay to go off alone with him and away from the group. It actually felt like I had known him before.
>
> When we arrived at the village, I remember that it felt familiar and inviting, but I have no recollection or sense of having lived there. It may have been different more than half a century ago, but now I have no recollection. What I remember about the village was the church and very vividly a stone wall

where we sat as we talked and rested. It was indeed a memorable twenty-four hours.

Barbara never returned to Bermuda and was unaware that the village was destroyed in 1780 until John told her.

When John contacted me eight years ago and shared his findings, I could relate fully to this since I have been interested in past, present, and future lives through most of my adult life, which was contrary to my family upbringing as a Christian. Recently I have been studying the Buddhist perspective on past lives. It confirms my beliefs. The fact that there are many others who have also had experiences of past lives is also very affirming. Direct experience has a lot to say about reality/realities.

Upon reflection, Barbara says that some of the events of her life now seem more understandable considering what John learned about the woman she might have been in the 18th century.

I've had many dreams throughout my life about being married in a small church. I never was married in a small church in this lifetime. I also have been unexplainably fearful and sometime in panic when swimming in deep water. I have always been a good swimmer in this life and would swim laps daily in three feet of water. If I would go to the deep end of a pool or lake, I would start feeling very anxious.

Yet I have always been drawn to the ocean and the waves and have found the rolling waves particularly calming. However, I would never get onto a cruise ship, even if it offered the world to me. I like having the earth under my feet. So when John said I drowned during a hurricane in Bermuda, it resonated with my attraction as well as my panic.

John and Barbara are both married for the second time. They have stayed in touch throughout the past eight years, but have never met face-to-face since Thanksgiving Day in 1964.

Neither seem like people who would make up a story about time travel. John, a North Carolinian, spent eight years in the Coast Guard and at age 24 became one of the youngest chief petty officers. After his service, he moved into the burgeoning computer field as a programmer and a technical manager. He later worked for a major long-distance carrier and developed national and international standards for the telecommunications industry. He retired in 2002 and has six grown children and five grandchildren.

Barbara, who resides in Minnesota and prefers not to use her last name, graduated in 1966 with a bachelor of science degree in nursing. After several years working as a nurse, she received a master's degree in nursing. She continued nursing and authored a book about infection control in nursing homes. In 1984, she went to law school and became a lawyer in 1988. For the next nine years, she primarily defended doctors and hospitals in malpractice suits. In 1997, she became the owner, administrator, and primary caregiver in a venture caring for the disabled. She continues this work, the most rewarding in her life. She has one son from her first marriage and two step-sons from her current marriage.

Of course, we can't help but wonder what would happen if John and Barbara returned to Bermuda and ventured again to the village site.

Chapter
3

Triangulating the Mystery

When Leonardo da Vinci was a young man, he met a strikingly beautiful woman whose presence left him dazzled. Even though he never saw her again, he knew that someday he would paint her portrait. But only from his memory. According to the story, da Vinci spent 10 or 15 minutes two or three times a day visualizing the woman and mentally painting her image. He did so for more than 30 years before he put her portrait to canvas. By then, he had a perfect image of her as if she were sitting in front of him posing for her portrait. The painting, of course, was one of da Vinci's most famous and celebrated works: the *Mona Lisa*.

I heard that story a few weeks before I encountered the Bermuda Triangle phenomenon. It was part of an episode of a BBC documentary series called *The Ascent of Man.* After my flight, I knew something unusual had happened to me. I vowed to remember every detail and began using the da Vinci method of daily focusing. So by 1996, when I made my first television appearance, I knew every detail of that flight by heart. After all, I had been visualizing every minute of it for 26 years.

At first, I didn't talk to anyone about the flight because it didn't make sense. I didn't know how to explain it. I couldn't figure it out, but I kept reviewing it every day. Then, 14 months after that flight, I saw two writers, Vincent Gaddis and Ivan Sanderson, on the *Dick Cavett Show* talking about a mysterious area of the Atlantic off the coast of

Florida. That was when I heard the term "Bermuda Triangle" for the first time and suddenly I was able to place my experience in a framework. Others had also encountered something very unusual in that region; and now it had a name.

I found out that Gaddis created the term "Bermuda Triangle" for an article in *Argosy Magazine* in 1964. In the story, he noted that numerous ships and planes had disappeared without explanation. Even earlier, in 1952, George X. Sands pointed out that an unusually large number of mysterious disappearances had occurred in that region. The first book on the subject, *Limbo of the Lost*, by John Wallace Spencer, was published in 1969, and two years later a documentary, *The Devil's Triangle*, was released.

In the interview, Sanderson touched on some of the possible explanations for the disappearances, including the idea of time travel. That was a momentous moment for me. How had we arrived 28 minutes ahead of schedule when it was impossible to travel that fast? We flew into a tunnel in the cloud near Bimini, and came out of the haze four minutes later near Miami. Was that the result of time travel? Had I entered a space-time warp? It seemed like it to me.

About the time I learned about the Bermuda Triangle, interest in the subject ballooned, and during the early 1970s there was an explosion in books on the subject. The most famous of them was Charles Berlitz's *The Bermuda Triangle*, which sold more than five million copies. One story most of the books include is the earliest reported sighting of strange phenomena in the waters at the edge of the Bermuda Triangle.

Back to Columbus

There was no such term as the "Bermuda Triangle" when Christopher Columbus sailed into the Sargasso Sea in the middle of the North Atlantic, southeast of Bermuda. The Sargasso Sea is the only sea without a coastline, but when Columbus and his crew saw birds and masses of floating seaweed, they thought they must be near land.

They sailed on through for days in light winds at best, but found no land. However, they encountered mysteries that would later become familiar elements of stories about the Bermuda Triangle. Columbus wrote in his logbook three times about erratic compass readings. He reported a dancing light on the horizon—even though they were too far out to see any fires on an island. He also noted that his crew was turning fearful.

We now know that Columbus wasn't the first European to reach the Americas. There is documented evidence of Norse explorers arriving in the 11th century. No doubt others, some possibly from Polynesia, journeyed to the Americas long before Columbus. But it seems we can say that Columbus was the first explorer to describe unusual events in the Bermuda Triangle.

Manson Valentine

Probably the person who was most influential in bringing my story to the public was Dr. Manson Valentine, director of the Miami Museum of Science. Dr. Valentine, who died in 1996 at the age of 92, had PhDs in zoology, paleontology, and geology, all from Yale. In spite of his academic background, Valentine was willing to explore so-called "fringe" subjects that many academic avoided, including Atlantis, UFOs, and the Bermuda Triangle. In fact, Charles Berlitz made extensive use of Valentine's research on the Bermuda Triangle for both of his books on the subject.

I learned of Valentine's interest in the subject when I saw him interviewed on a television news program three years after my experience. As he started talking, something extraordinary happened: The television screen disappeared and I saw another image. My eyes were open and I felt very excited. It was extraordinary, because I saw Dr.

Valentine and myself and both our wives dining together at a water-front restaurant, and we seemed to be friends.

As a result of the vision, I called Valentine's office and left a message. A week later, Valentine called me back and we agreed to meet at Valentine's home in downtown Miami, a well-kept older home that belonged to another era of Miami, but now was surrounded by high-rise buildings.

At first, we conducted a normal conversation at a table with Valentine asking me several questions about the weather conditions and situation leading up to my flight. But when I started describing the flight itself, Valentine's behavior shifted. I noticed that his eyes started closing. As I continued to explain the details of the flight, he slowly lowered his head until it rested on his forearms on the tabletop.

This startled me, as I thought something was wrong. I turned to his wife, Anna, who told me in a quiet voice not to worry, that he was going into a trance, and that he could still hear me. It felt strange telling my story to someone who appeared to be asleep, but I later came to understand that the reason he was in a trance-like state was so that he could attain a higher level of concentration to analyze my flight. I had the feeling that he was visualizing the same images that I was seeing in my mind as I spoke.

I continued to talk for close to 30 minutes and he never moved a muscle. It was as if he had fallen into a very deep sleep. When I finished, Dr. Valentine slowly raised his head, then opened his eyes. He looked at me, smiled, turned to Anna, and said: "This is amazing. He is the only pilot to have ever flown through the heart of the storm, from its birth through its maturity and to exit through the vortex."

Valentine thought that the Bermuda Triangle and Atlantis were connected. The link, he believed, was UFOs, which he thought might be vehicles for time travelers moving through inter-dimensional portals in the Bermuda Triangle between Atlantis and our world—or other worlds and other dimensions. After our meeting, Valentine and his wife, Anna, took my wife, Lynn, and me to dinner at a waterfront restaurant—amazingly, the same one I had seen in the vision!

Several months after I met Dr. Valentine, he invited me to a small gathering that included Charles Berlitz, whose book on the Triangle was on the best-seller's list. At one point in the evening Valentine and Berlitz took me aside and I told Berlitz my story. He took notes as Valentine questioned me and guided me through the story that he now knew well. Berlitz was fascinated by what he heard and included my story in his follow-up book, *Without a Trace*. At the end of the evening Valentine surprised me with his parting comment: "You must always remember that you hold the key to the Bermuda Triangle."

It seemed very significant to him that I should understand that. But I was a kid in my 20s, and I just couldn't imagine that I held the key to something so utterly awesome and mysterious.

Early Memories

I actually had heard a Bermuda Triangle story before my experience, but at the time I didn't know it was related to a mysterious phenomenon. I had been flying off the coast of Florida for about five years before my encounter with the "time storm" and the tunnel vortex. During those years, nothing unusual had happened to me.

I was working in the building development business with my dad in 1965 when I was 19, and soon after that I got involved in real estate with two family friends, step-brothers named Ford Carter and Don McKinney. They became my aviation mentors, as both were highly qualified pilots. They owned a Twin Bonanza and had made more than 500 flights to the Bahamas developing and selling real estate. They were the first developers of the island of Providenciales in the Turks and Caicos Islands located southeast of the Bahamas.

Ford was about 45 years old and Don was about 55. Don, in particular, was like a father figure to me. I was in awe of him because he was a retired Air Force pilot, a highly decorated colonel, who had flown the famous Boeing B-29 Superfortress, the plane that carried the nuclear bomb that ended the war. He was General Jimmy Doolittle's back-up bomber flying in formation flight with an extra atomic bomb aboard his B-29 in case Doolittle had problems dropping the bombs on Nagasaki and Hiroshima.

Don and Ford's real estate office was located in Delray Beach, where I worked with them, and often I would go to lunch with them and several other associates. Through the years, they mentioned several times an experience they had flying in the Bahamas. I could tell it was something very special because they would both get excited. Little did I know that their story was about an encounter with the Bermuda Triangle phenomenon, and that my own experience would take place in the same area southeast of Andros Island.

On that day, they departed Palm Beach with two airplanes flying direct to Provo. Ford was flying his Twin Bonanza and Don was copilot in a Lear Jet flown by one of their investors. Ford took off first and leveled off at around 10,000 feet. Don departed about an hour later on the same flight path, but cruised at 45,000 feet.

After Ford got over Andros he contacted Don on the radio and found that they weren't far behind. He told them he saw a strange storm offshore of his flight path and it had no ceiling. He couldn't fly over it so he was going to try to fly around it. Soon after, Don and copilot Richard Dupont saw the storm and realized it was even too high for them to fly over. Richard wanted to fly through it, but Don wouldn't let him. It was one of the only times he was frightened in an airplane. He said there was a strange ring around the storm and the ring appeared to be rising upward from the ocean surface. He said he had never seen anything like it before and it reminded him of an atomic bomb going off, like the one he actually witnessed in Japan.

They both managed to make it around the storm and land at Provo. It was something they could never forget and they were glad they didn't end up inside the strange storm. I remember their experience well, but I never really thought about it while flying in the Bahamas. It wasn't until more than six years later that I realized they had seen something similar to what I flew through. Once I realized I had experienced an extraordinary event related to a great mystery within this area, I started telling everyone I knew—and anyone who would listen—about my experience.

Don heard about my experience second-hand. One Sunday afternoon while I was visiting my parents, he barged in unannounced and said he wanted to talk to Dad and me. He had a completely different attitude than normal. He usually was very cheerful, but this time he seemed dead serious. We sat down at the dinner table and he grilled us for close to two hours. He acted as if he was an Air Force Jag attorney. He wanted to know every detail of the flight and he wanted to see if my dad would back up my story. My dad was the copilot and he verified everything I said.

Don finally ended the interrogation and seemed to believe us. Then his attitude changed and he proceeded to tell us a story that he had kept to himself for years. One day during the late 1950s, he was flying a P-51 Mustang fighter plane and said he encountered a flying saucer. It flew right by him so he decided to chase it. He fired his guns at it, but it had no effect. The vehicle quickly accelerated away at a fantastic speed and disappeared out of sight.

At the time, the government's policy was to engage UFOs. Later, during the Cold War era, it seems a decision was made to alter that policy, according to Richard Dolan, author of *UFOs and the National Security State,* after it became clear we were powerless against them. "At this point, the U.S. government seemed to change its attitude to observing UFOs."

Many years after *THE FOG* was published, Ford Carter called me after reading it, and told me a story that he considered to be the strangest event he ever had flying in the Bahamas. He was flying from

Florida to Provo and, as he approached Andros Island, he encountered a series of thunderstorms. He had already avoided several of them when two adjacent storms appeared ahead of him. They were linked at the top, forming a bridge that was about three miles long, a thousand feet above the sea, and a thousand feet wide.

Ford aimed for the bridge, planning to fly under it and escape the storms. But he noticed something strange as he approached the bridge. The underside on either end was flat, forming 90-degree angles. It took about a minute to fly under the bridge and the sides remained perfectly flat—rather than curved like typical clouds connecting two storms. He continued onward to Provo and, after he landed, he couldn't stop talking about what he had just witnessed.

That story was significant because it seemingly is supported by events in an episode of the Science Channel's *What on Earth?*. The episode focused on a satellite view of unusual cloud formations over the Bahamas. The clouds had flat sides and formed hexagons. Each side of the hexagon looked to be about 15 miles long, forming a hexagon with an inside diameter of about 25 miles and an outside diameter of about 45 miles. This is about the same size as the time storm I flew through.

One of the meteorologists on the show mentioned that it is very rare in meteorology for clouds to form right angles. Of course, most clouds have curved edges and that's why Ford's encounter was so unusual. But when a snowflake is magnified, we see many geometric shapes. There might be a parallel on a larger scale with clouds under certain conditions.

"Mysterious Universe"

In the early 1990s, documentary producers started to take an interest in the Bermuda Triangle, and they contacted me after reading about my story in Charles Berlitz's second book on the subject, *Without a Trace*. In spite of the passage of years, I still clearly remembered what happened on the flight because I was still replaying it in my mind every day. The first television interview I did was with *Arthur C. Clarke's Mysterious Universe.*

Just as I'd foreseen myself spending time with Manson Valentine, I had a vision in 1992 that I would be going on television to talk about my story. I was driving in the Florida Keys, where I lived, along the Overseas Highway. I had just reached the apex of one of the three bridges connecting Upper Matecumbe and Lower Matecumbe when a sudden sensation of excitement rippled through me. I knew that I was about to experience something unusual, and I was concerned because driving down the highway at 55 miles per hour and having a vision is not a good idea.

I was only a few miles from my home and concentrated on my driving. As soon as I pulled into my carport, I turned off the engine and started to relax. My body went limp and slumped in my seat. I turned my body slightly to the left and looked down on to the gray carport floor. I felt like I was floating on a cloud and looking down into a gray abyss.

I kept my eyes open even though it seemed like I was dreaming. Suddenly, a vision appeared before me and I could see it crystal clear. It was like watching a television screen that was playing a movie. After a few moments, I realized that the television was part of the vision. I was watching an elderly man with gray, thinning hair and glasses, who seemed to be the host of a television show. He looked familiar, but I didn't recognize him.

Then I saw myself on the screen and realized that the man was introducing me. Maybe it was a fantasy, but it seemed that the man was giving me an opportunity to tell the world about my mysterious flight in 1970. The vision lasted nearly five minutes; besides the interview I saw myself flying around what appeared to be the Florida Keys in an unfamiliar airplane. When the vision faded, I felt elated, as if I had just awakened from a special dream.

In late 1994, nearly three years later, Granite Film & Television Productions contacted me. They told me that Arthur C. Clarke wanted me to appear on his television series, *Arthur C. Clarke's Mysterious Universe.* That was when I realized that I had already seen the show in my vision.

The film crew arrived from London several weeks later. They used my airplane, which I had purchased the year prior, to film the aerial shots. The program appeared on the Discovery Channel and was called *Squaring the Bermuda Triangle.* Everything that I can remember from the vision, including a new airplane, was very much like the television show.

As of mid-2016, I have appeared on nearly three dozen documentaries about the Bermuda Triangle. But how was it possible for me to see something that would take place several years in the future? Did it have anything to do with my experience in the cloud and the fog? Hard to say. All I know is that prior to that flight through the tunnel vortex and into the fog, I never had any such visions.

They Still Remember

Some people might think it odd that I'm still talking about something that happened to me on a flight nearly 50 years ago. That's why it's very encouraging when I receive email from others who had somewhat similar experiences many years ago and have never forgotten about them. The following are two such stories.

Although these are one-source stories, that doesn't mean they're not true. I tend to believe that something mysterious happened to both of these men, and that they didn't just decide to make up a story and send it to me for no conceivable reason.

The first is from Roland, a former professional pilot, who retired from flying a few years ago. His story dates back four decades, but it is an event he still clearly recalls.

"Back in 1978, I flew from Bimini to Opa-Locka in my 1977 Skyhawk. I was a flight instructor, but was just flying for my own personal fun. I had flown in and out of the Bahamas about a dozen times and was competent and confident."

Roland was 20 years old at the time and initially the event he experienced didn't have a huge impact on him. "My 'vortex experience' is not as dramatic as the one you had. But there are so many similarities that I simply needed to contact you."

On his return from Bimini, he was flying at about 10,000 feet with 10 miles of visibility in haze. "It was summer. All was normal. Then we got a call from Miami Approach that radar contact was lost. I didn't give it much thought, figuring that a small cell had moved between the radar antenna and our position. Then we lost radio contact. We couldn't hear or transmit. And a minute later, the compass—a regular Cessna 'whiskey compass'—began doing three-sixties! The air was smooth, but the sky was gray, hazy and weird."

Roland wrote that he had never experienced anything like that before—or since. "The compass was new, just like the airplane. I had bought the Skylark brand new and was the only one who had flown it. Besides that, I was impeccable with every single aspect of maintenance."

He held his heading as best he could and felt mildly uncomfortable about their situation. That wasn't the case, however, with his passenger in the right seat. "He was a private pilot with about 200 hours and he was freaking out!"

Roland said the entire experience lasted about 10 minutes. "I had a strange sensation that made no sense to me at the time, but I just blew it all off." To distract himself from the odd sensation, he talked to his friend about how they had briefly disappeared into the Bermuda Triangle. "Today, I recognize the feeling I had as the same sensation I've experienced at special vortex sites, such as sacred sites in Peru. But this was quite intense."

Eventually, the radio came back, the compass settled down, and everything was normal again. They flew on without further incident. However, Roland noted that he never forgot what happened on that flight. "I really felt a need to share this with you. I've kept fairly quiet about the whole thing over the decades, just chalking it up as something that went unexplained. I believe now that I'm extremely lucky to be here today."

Something very similar happened to Jeff Butler, a professional pilot living in St. Augustine, Florida. He writes: "I happened to catch a few minutes of a program on Discovery featuring your experience. It caught me off-guard because I had a similar experience while flying a Piper Seneca from Naples to Marathon, Florida, in 1999."

Jeff was flying at night and was accompanied by another experienced pilot, who was talking to Miami Radio when they entered a cloud layer "that came out of nowhere." Even though the air was smooth, he recalls: "All at once our gyros went out of whack and our GPS failed. We figured we were about thirty miles north of Marathon. My partner tried to contact Miami, but had no response. We tried several back-up frequencies with no luck."

They flew for another five to 10 minutes shrouded by the same cloud cover. Finally, they emerged into clear air and "all at once everything returned to normal and we re-established contact with Miami. They told us they had lost radar contact with us and had been trying to call the entire time. We experienced nothing unusual after that."

A Yellow Mist

An even stranger story comes from Jon, another correspondent who encountered the fog while aboard a commercial jetliner. This was the first high-altitude fog experience we've heard about. It happened long ago, but Jon thinks about it often. He is particularly fascinated by my teleportation/time-travel experience.

"I have followed your story for years and am convinced there is a history about the Earth that includes a past where people and objects could and did transport completely off the planet to other places and worlds. I also had a similar experience in the Bermuda Triangle."

As a boy, Jon would spend his summers sailing and exploring the Caribbean Islands with his father aboard his Vintage Gaff Rigged Schooner. By summer's end, he would board a commercial jet and return to the States, usually without incident. However, in August of 1976, while approaching the Bahamas, Jon's flight experienced a bizarre turn of events.

> While your flight was at 10,000 feet, we were flying at 36,000 feet and traveling at 500 knots. The weather was clear and I could see for at least fifty miles on either side of the aircraft. There were no weather issues of any type, just scattered cumulus clouds below and purple sky above. Then suddenly, out of nowhere, the plane was shadowed by a bright yellow mist. Soon it completely enveloped the 747.

After about 20 minutes, the commercial jet escaped the fog. But Jon's watch seemingly had stopped and so had everyone else's. It was as if no time had passed while the plane was in the fog. When the fog disappeared, the watches began working again. But they were all 20 minutes behind. "Before we landed, the pilot told us to reset our watches to the correct time," he recalled.

But that wasn't the end of the experience. "What happened after we landed in Miami was really interesting. After the plane touched down ...the pilot said he had been instructed to taxi to the back of the airport where the customs gate was located, and we would deplane there."

When they arrived, a host of people were waiting for them and it wasn't friends and family members of the passengers.

> As the plane pulled up to this area, there were several unusual looking vehicles nearby and men in suits. A host of people

with cameras and electronic devices I'd never seen before were spread out over the tarmac, the cameras and instruments set up on tripods. One man began walking around the plane with what looked like a Geiger Counter. Another group of people began checking the wing fuel tanks. We were required to remain seated until officials came aboard and allowed us to leave the plane.

Jon made inquiries later and a mechanic for Eastern Airlines passed along a rumor that planes flying through the Bermuda Triangle occasionally would go missing from radar. It supposedly was something that was being kept secret and pilots were not allowed to talk about it.

Even though nearly four decades have passed since his experience, Jon has never forgotten about that strange yellow mist and how it seemingly froze time. He says he would like to contact others who were on that flight. The pilots probably didn't report the shift in time. Making such a comment in the flight log could have resulted in concerns about their mental stability. They could have been grounded and required to undergo mental and physical exams. But after all these years, it would be interesting to hear the story of that flight from the pilots, as well as other passengers.

chapter 4

The Lore of Flight 19

It was a mystery and a tragedy, one that claimed 27 lives and was responsible for the disappearance of six airplanes—all in one day from the same base. There was no combat, no enemy, no war. Yet, December 5, 1945, became a black day in the annals of military aviation, and a cornerstone in a larger mystery that has claimed thousands of aircraft and vessels throughout the centuries.

Five Navy torpedo bombers with 14 crew members on a routine training mission from their base in Fort Lauderdale vanished, and a rescue craft with a crew of 13 was swallowed in the same mysterious event. Instead of gunfire, as in time of war, it was a case of disorientation triggered by the mysterious spinning of compasses, according to the Navy's 500-page report on the tragedy.

Even those who have thoroughly researched the mystery of Flight 19 probably have never heard about the uncanny connection of the flight to the number 23. But I'm jumping ahead. First, here's my take on the flight to oblivion.

The Mission

In spite of the massive interest the flight has generated, initially it was as ordinary as the 18 flights from the base that had preceded it that day. That's why it was labeled Flight 19. Although it has been called the Lost Squadron or Lost Patrol by the press, it wasn't patrolling anything, just flying a triangular-shaped practice run from the Fort Lauderdale Naval Air Station to the Bahamas and back. The flight was scheduled to last two hours and 15 minutes and extend no further than 123 miles from the base. Considered the Navy's best bombing planes for destroying submarines, the sturdy TBM Avengers could carry 2,000 pounds of bombs and fly for 1,000 miles on a tank of fuel. If there were any problem, they were supposed to fly directly west to Florida, according to the Navy's exhaustive report.

If Flight 19 had returned home safely, I suspect that the Bermuda Triangle might never have gained the notoriety that it has today. It would be regarded as an area in which strange things sometimes happened, an area of deadly storms and puzzling electromagnetic anomalies that caused equipment failures. But in the years that followed the loss of Flight 19, researchers gathered stories of other lost planes and boats, and noted a confluence of disappearances. As a result, the Bermuda Triangle became a state of mind for unlucky happenings as well as a label for an area of mystery and treachery.

The infamous flight, as described by the Navy report, began with the takeoff of the five torpedo bombers at 2:10 p.m. The route formed a triangle: east to the Berry Islands, then north to an island near Grand Bahama Island, then back to Fort Lauderdale. Two similar squadrons had completed the exercise earlier in the day and another one had left just 25 minutes ahead of Flight 19. None of the other squadrons experienced any difficulties. This flight, however, would turn into something extraordinary. The lead pilot, Commander Charles Taylor, would become disoriented, he would radio that his compasses had failed, and he would become convinced that they were impossibly off course. All five planes and all 14 airmen would vanish without a trace.

Spinning Compasses

The first sign of trouble was recorded at 3:40 p.m., an hour and a half into the flight. They had conducted their planned bombing practice at Chicken and Hen Shoals, headed farther east, then turned northwest. If they continued on that course, they would have arrived at the mainland on schedule. But something was wrong with Taylor. He seemed confused about their location. Taylor was a veteran of combat in the South Pacific and had been flying since 1941, so this was out of the ordinary.

Lieutenant Michael Cox, a senior instructor at the naval air station, who was also flying at the time, overheard Taylor asking his second-in-command for help on the squadron's assigned radio frequency. Cox later told the naval board of investigators that Taylor kept asking Marine Captain Edward J. Powers, Jr. what his compass read. Finally, Taylor admitted he was lost. "I don't know where we are," he radioed the other pilots, a transmission picked up by Cox. "We must have got lost after that last turn."

Cox contacted Taylor on the radio and asked what was wrong. Taylor replied: "Both my compasses are out and I'm trying to find Fort Lauderdale. I'm over land, but it's broken. I'm sure I'm in the keys, but I don't know how far down and I don't know how to get to Fort Lauderdale."

In retrospect, it seems that something was affecting Taylor's thinking as well as his instruments. That's my opinion, as well as the one expressed by Navy investigators in their report. Taylor had been based in Key West and was familiar with the area. Any pilot with even a fraction of his experience flying in the keys would know that reaching Fort Lauderdale would simply require following the chain of islands to the mainland with the afternoon sun to the rear and left of the plane.

Cox told Taylor to put the sun on his port wing and fly up the coast until he reached Fort Lauderdale. "What's your present altitude? I'll fly down and meet you."

After a moment, Taylor replied, "I know where I am now. I'm at 2,300 feet. Don't come after me."

"Roger, you're at 2,300. I'm coming to meet you anyhow," Cox answered. But Cox told Navy investigators that he never found the five Avengers flying in formation, because they weren't in the keys.

Although four of the five pilots of Flight 19 were students in a training program, they were all experienced with an average of 400 hours of flying time. Their next assignment was to start landing on aircraft carriers, a task reserved for the Navy's more capable pilots. At 29 years old, Taylor was the senior pilot. He had accumulated 2,509 flight hours and the Navy considered him an excellent pilot. But on that day, nothing seemed to go right for Taylor.

While Cox headed south toward the keys, he heard Taylor again on the radio: "Can you have Miami or someone turn on their radar gear and pick us up? We don't seem to be getting far."

Taylor told Cox that one of the students was leading the squadron, but he became convinced during the second leg of the flight that they were off course, so he took over the lead. Cox recalled that Taylor saying: "I'm sure now that neither one of my compasses is working."

Cox contacted Taylor again, and this time Taylor wasn't at all certain of his location. He kept asking the other pilots in the squadron for compass headings, but the confusion remained. It seemed that none of the pilots were certain about their compasses. Was it possible that all the compasses were malfunctioning?

A few months after the tragic incident, the Navy released its report that initially faulted Taylor, but was later revised to "cause or reasons unknown" for the disappearance of the planes. Two decades later, as interest in the Bermuda Triangle peaked, the Navy again addressed the Flight 19 tragedy in an article that appeared in the June 1974 issue of *Sealift*. In it, Howard L. Rosenberg wrote: "If the planes were flying through a magnetic storm, all compasses could possibly malfunction. Actually, man's knowledge of magnetism is limited. We know how to live with it and escape it by going into space, but we really don't know what exactly it is."

Disorientation

Cox told Taylor to turn on his emergency IFF gear. When activated, it brightens the image on land-based radar screens. Taylor, in his confusion, said he didn't have an IFF. But later he located it and turned it on. Cox also told Taylor to turn on his ZBX, a homing device much like the automatic direction finders used in planes today, which tells the pilot which direction to steer. The Navy report also noted that three land-based naval operations also radioed Taylor telling him to turn on his ZBX. None received a reply.

At 4 p.m., Cox heard Taylor say that he was flying at 4,500 feet, and visibility was 10 to 12 miles. But the radio transmissions were fading and Cox was unable to contact Taylor again. Cox returned to Fort Lauderdale at 4:40 p.m. under worsening weather conditions as a storm moved in from the Atlantic. Cox heard one final transmission from Taylor in which he repeated that he had assumed the lead of the flight after the student pilots had headed in the wrong direction.

In studying Flight 19, I re-created the flight path followed by the squadron. The second checkpoint for the pilots was an island called Great Sale Cay, located about 20 miles north of Grand Bahama Island. Because they were heading north and the wind was increasing in intensity, they probably missed the island, passing it by 10 miles to the east. That's when Taylor, who thought he was in the keys and about to reach Miami, radioed: "We don't seem to be getting far."

Years after my own experience in the Bermuda Triangle, I flew a route similar to the one that Flight 19 had taken. Both I and my copilot, Chris Hope, had lived in the Florida Keys, and were amazed by the similarities between the Bahamas and the keys. Hope pointed out that one of the islands looked identical to Key Largo. We viewed the islands from different altitudes and the lower we went, the more they seemed to resemble the keys. In particular, a group of 20 islands between Grand Bahama and Little Abaco Island, known as the Cross Cays, looked like the islands in the lower keys surrounding Big Pine Key. The difference, of course, was that a series of bridges connect a string of keys. However, there are dozens of smaller keys that aren't connected by bridges.

Lieutenant Commander Charles M. Kenyon, station operations officer of the Fort Lauderdale Naval Air Station, told Navy investigators that he wasn't overly concerned when he heard about Flight 19's problems. Several other pilots had become disoriented in the past, and they all managed to find their way back to the base. Also, he recently lectured pilots on procedures to follow when planes become lost. He later told investigators: "I figured they were temporarily confused and with all the instructions we had given them, and with another plane in the air that had picked up the transmissions, they would come back right on time."

More Transmissions, More Confusion

At 4:25 p.m., personnel at the Port Everglades Radio picked up a transmission from Taylor. "We've just passed over a small island. We have no other land in sight. I'm at altitude 3,500 feet. Have on emergency IFF. Does anyone in the area have a radar screen that could pick us up?"

At that point, I think the squadron was passing over the barrier islands beyond Great Abaco Island. The islands are about 10 miles apart, so they could fly for a short time without seeing land. The Navy report detailed flight maneuvers, their times, and comments picked up by radio receivers.

At 4:30 p.m., Port Everglades Radio made contact with Taylor again. Because Taylor was having problems with his compass, they suggested that he let one of the other pilots lead the way back. Taylor acknowledged the suggestion, then a few minutes later he said that one of the pilots thought if they headed west, they would reach the mainland.

At 4:45 p.m., Taylor contacted Port Everglades and said: "We're heading 030 degrees [north-northeast] for 45 minutes; then we will fly north to make sure we are not over the Gulf of Mexico."

At around 5 p.m., one of the student pilots told Taylor: "If we just fly west, we would get home." Another of the student pilots agreed. "Damn it, if we would just fly west...."

You might wonder why the two pilots didn't break off from the others and fly west to save their lives. Although they questioned Taylor, they remained committed to the mission. Military pilots are rigorously trained to follow the lead of their commander—no matter what. Breaking that rule would probably have ended their careers. As it happened, following the code of conduct in that case had even more dire consequences.

In spite of the urgent messages from the two pilots, it is clear that Taylor still believed they were over the Gulf of Mexico. He was heard telling the pilots to continue north for 10 minutes. Then several minutes later, he said, "We're going too damn far north instead of east. If there is anything, we would've seen it."

Then Taylor radioed the mainland again. "Hello, Port Everglades, this is Flight 19. Do you read? Over."

"Flight 19, this is Port Everglades. Go ahead."

"I receive you very weak. We are now heading west," he reported at 5:15.

At about that time, Taylor was heard telling all the planes to join up and continue in formation. If any plane had to ditch, they would all ditch together. Five minutes later, he said, "When the first man gets down to 10 gallons of gas, we will all land in the water together. Does everyone understand that?"

Taylor's comments show his continued confusion and his growing anxiety. He was already talking about ditching in deep water. Chances of a night rescue would be slim. The sun was setting in about 10 minutes. It was cloudy and there would be no moon. Yet they should have had more than two hours of fuel left—more than enough to make it back to the island they had flown over.

"Port Everglades, this is Taylor. I receive you very weak. How is the weather over Lauderdale?"

"Weather over Lauderdale is clear. Over Key West CAVU (ceiling and visibility unlimited). Over the Bahamas—cloudy, rather low ceiling, poor visibility."

It would be pitch black outside the cockpit within half an hour. The ocean was rough because of the strong winds. Why they continued flying over deep water, instead of returning to the island that they had seen with the past hour, baffles me. If they ditched in shallow water near shore, they would have a strong chance of surviving.

At about 6 p.m., Port Everglades called Taylor. "Did you receive my last transmission Change to 3,000 kilocycles?"

"I cannot change frequency," Taylor replied. "I must keep my planes intact. Cannot change to 3,000 kilocycles, will stay on 4,805 kilocycles."

Once again, Taylor was forgetting his training. An important part of the lost plane procedure is to change to the emergency frequency. The transmissions would come over the radio stronger, and there would be many more stations on the ground that would be able to hear them and be capable of replying and offering assistance. Taylor should have switched to the emergency frequency two hours earlier.

By 6 p.m., Flight 19 had been heading west for approximately 45 minutes. When they made the turn, they were probably about 90 miles east-northeast of the barrier islands of the Abacos that Taylor had mistaken for the Florida Keys. Now their location would be about 50 miles north of Walkers Cay, the northernmost Bahama Island. They would be more than a hundred miles off the Florida coast and would be able to reach the coastline in less than an hour.

By 6:02, Port Everglades was picking up fragments of conversations between the pilots. But none of the pilots could hear their calls.

In fact, there were numerous blackouts when no transmissions were heard, then the voices would be received again. Gian Quasar in *Into the Bermuda Triangle* notes: "The mystery of where their compasses were directing them is compounded by the mystery of radio reception. The signals were strangely erratic: clear one moment, they faded to barely audible the next moment, died out altogether, or were obscured by heavy static."

The Navy report documented the final messages. "We may have to ditch at any moment," a voice said.

"Taylor to Powers. Do you read?...Taylor to Powers. I've been trying to reach you. Holding west course."

But then in another puzzling development, Taylor reversed himself again. "We didn't go far enough east. Turn around again We may just as well turn around and go east again... This is Taylor. Turn around fly east until we run out of gas. I think we would have a better chance of being picked up close to shore."

"Taylor, this is Port Everglades. Do you read me?"

Unidentified voice: "Negative.... What course are we on?" "We are over the Gulf. We didn't go far enough east.... How long have we been on this course?"

Unidentified voice: "What course are we on now?"

After 6:17, only garbled transmissions were heard. Their voices became weaker and, by 7:04, Flight 19 was silent.

At the time Taylor suggested they turn east again, the squadron would have been about 70 miles east of Florida. By that time it was dark, with a broken cloud ceiling from 800 to 1,200 feet, with scattered showers. The wind was picking up out of the west-southwest, gusting to 30 miles per hour. They would have been over the Gulf Stream, where the waves were building on the rough seas.

If they had maintained their westerly heading, they would have reached Florida before 7 p.m. Unfortunately, the squadron apparently took Taylor's bizarre suggestion to fly east until they ran out of gas. They would have vanished into the abyss of the Sargasso Sea.

The Search

Five Navy seaplanes were dispatched shortly after 6 p.m. About 10 ships in the search area were also alerted. Minutes earlier, ComGulf Sea Frontiers Evaluation Center in Miami had vectored the approximate position of Flight 19. To obtain this position, the center used directional bearings that were sent from stations along the coastline from New Jersey to Texas. The position fix was quoted as being within a hundred-mile radius of 29 degrees, 15 minutes north, 79 degrees, 00 minutes west. That would be about 225 miles northeast of Fort Lauderdale, about 150 to 200 miles off the east coast of Florida.

The search planes were handicapped by the darkness and stormy weather. No trace of the five Avengers was found. Adding to the mystery, one of the search planes, a PBM Mariner—a large military craft sometimes referred to as a "flying boat"—with 13 crew members also vanished into what would become known as the Bermuda Triangle. No bodies were ever found from the Avengers or the Mariner. However, one of the search ships saw an enormous fireball on the horizon, indicating that the fuel in the plane had exploded just 20 minutes into the flight.

The next day, one of the largest searches in history started at sunrise. More than 200 planes and 17 ships joined the search for the missing airmen. The search area extended 300 miles east into the Atlantic and north and south along the entire state. By sunset, no trace of Flight 19 had been found. The next day, 242 planes continued the search and additional ships joined those already prowling the seas for the lost squadron. Again, nothing was found. The effort continued for three more days.

On the fifth day, at 3:27 p.m., a message was sent from the Miami evaluation center to all the planes, ships, and stations: "Search for five missing planes on December 5, 1945, will be terminated on completion of the return of all planes on the mission today. No further special search is contemplated. All planes and vessels in the area keep a bright lookout and report any pertinent information."

The search for Flight 19 was over. The men were all assumed dead. But the controversy about the reasons for the disappearance was just beginning.

Although the Navy wasn't able to pinpoint the location of the lost flight, I believe the squadron ditched their planes about 90 miles eastnortheast of the barrier islands of the Abacos, which Taylor had mistaken for the keys.

The Investigation

In January 1946, the Miami Naval Board of Investigation issued its final report on the case: "The primary reason for the disappearance of Flight 19 was the confusion of the flight leader as to his location, his failure to take into account the strong winds, which apparently carried him farther east than he realized, and his failure to utilize radio aids which were available to him."

Rear Admiral F.D. Wagner added a final note to the report: "The leaders of the flight became so hopelessly confused as to have suffered something akin to a mental aberration."

Charles Taylor's mother, Katherine Taylor, and her sister, Mary Carroll, were unhappy with the board's final report. They started a campaign urging the board to reconsider their decision to place the

Abaco Island in the Bahamas (top two) looks very similar to the Florida Keys (bottom two), a possible cause for the confusion among Flight 19 pilots, who were used to flying in the keys. Photo credit: Bruce Gernon.

blame on Lieutenant Taylor. To that end, the family located a young attorney named William L.P. Burke. He was the ideal lawyer to defend the defamed pilot. The reason? Taylor had saved Burke's life twice while they were stationed together in Key West. The first time, Taylor flew a seaplane into the Bahamas and landed in a storm to save Burke, who was adrift on a life raft after a crash. Later, when Burke lost his way during a night flight, Taylor found him and escorted him back to the base.

Burke filed an appeal, asking the Navy to reconsider the Taylor case. On November 19, 1947, the Board for Correction of Naval Records exonerated Taylor. "After careful and conscientious consideration of all the factors of the case, the board was of the opinion that the flight had disappeared for causes or reasons unknown."

Taylor was no longer blamed for the loss of Flight 19. But that didn't change the opinions of some investigators, who continued to claim Taylor was at fault. The missing planes have never been found, in spite of extensive mapping of the flight area in recent decades through the use of undersea photography and sonar.

Similar Storms

When I first heard about Flight 19 in 1971, I suspected that the squadron flew through an electromagnetic storm similar to the one I experienced. As a result, I've always felt closely associated with the lost pilots and realize how fortunate I was to avoid a similar fate.

I've read extensively about the flight, and today I still suspect that the pilots encountered the same unknown meteorological phenomenon. Possibly, the entire squadron flying in formation lost the use of their compasses and other electronic equipment. But in this case, the disorientation was so severe that the lead pilot thought he was flying over the Gulf of Mexico.

Weather conditions tend to repeat themselves in nearly identical form. For example, hurricane season is the same months each year.

A large thunderstorm may materialize at a certain location, and the next day a very similar storm appears there at the same time of day. A large cold front may traverse North America on a particular day in the winter, and years later a similar cold front will pass through on the same day or same week. A hurricane may travel from Africa and blast through the Caribbean, then turn north and dissipate in the Atlantic. Many years later, a similar hurricane may take the same path on the same days.

I believe a similar cyclical phenomenon occurred on December 5, 1945, and again on December 4, 1970, at the same location over the Great Bahama Bank. Both storms were born at around 3 p.m. and they died about 30 minutes later. Because of the speed in which the storm appears and disappears, it isn't noticed on radar. The storm I flew through was around 50 miles in diameter, which placed its northern extremity in the path of Flight 19.

I contend that Flight 19 entered this storm at about 3:30, and exited it less than 10 minutes later just before Charles Taylor made his first distress call. My guess is that Flight 19 penetrated too deeply into the storm and into a field of electromagnetic energy. By staying within the storm for close to 10 minutes, they were overexposed to the electromagnetic energy, which had a dramatic effect on the outcome of their flight.

An encounter with "electronic fog" (what I call such experiences), could account for the confusion that apparently affected lead pilot Taylor and other crew members. That's what happened on my December 1970 flight, not to me, but to my passengers. My father, a seasoned pilot, became hysterical when Miami Control told us there were no airplanes on the radar near Bimini. His business partner, Chuck Layfayette, also acted odd. His voice was slurred and he was babbling nonsensically. But after we landed he was fine.

Although there is no definitive proof that Flight 19 entered an electromagnetic storm, or that such a storm could affect the minds of the pilots, we know that storm conditions were present during the flight, that both of Taylor's compasses had malfunctioned, and that his thinking seemed illogical. He was confused and disoriented. When they passed over the Cross Cay Islands near Abaco, Taylor thought he recognized the Florida Keys and couldn't shake the idea, in spite of evidence to the contrary.

However, I don't think that Taylor can be blamed for the disappearance of the planes. He had no record of mental aberrations and he was

The memorial dedicated to all aviators who flew at Naval Air Station Fort Lauderdale.
Photo credit: Bruce Gernon.

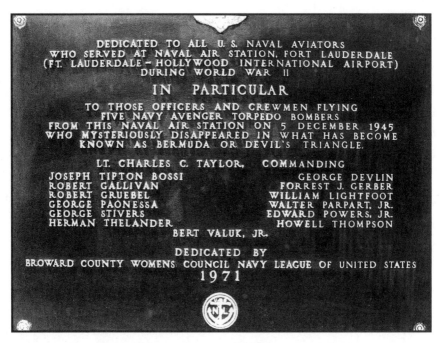

DEDICATED TO ALL U. S. NAVAL AVIATORS
WHO SERVED AT NAVAL AIR STATION, FORT LAUDERDALE
(FT. LAUDERDALE – HOLLYWOOD INTERNATIONAL AIRPORT)
DURING WORLD WAR II

IN   PARTICULAR

TO THOSE OFFICERS AND CREWMEN FLYING
FIVE NAVY AVENGER TORPEDO BOMBERS
FROM THIS NAVAL AIR STATION ON 5 DECEMBER 1945
WHO MYSTERIOUSLY DISAPPEARED IN WHAT HAS BECOME
KNOWN AS BERMUDA OR DEVIL'S TRIANGLE.

LT. CHARLES C. TAYLOR,   COMMANDING

JOSEPH TIPTON BOSSI
ROBERT GALLIVAN
ROBERT GRUEBEL
GEORGE PAONESSA
GEORGE STIVERS
HERMAN THELANDER

GEORGE DEVLIN
FORREST J. GERBER
WILLIAM LIGHTFOOT
WALTER PARPART, JR.
EDWARD POWERS, JR.
HOWELL THOMPSON

BERT VALUK, JR.

DEDICATED BY
BROWARD COUNTY WOMENS COUNCIL NAVY LEAGUE OF UNITED STATES
1971

The plaque at the memorial specifically honors officers and crewmen flying five Navy Avenger Torpedo Bombers from this Naval Air Station on December 5, 1945. Photo credit: Bruce Gernon.

a distinguished Navy pilot. If everything had been normal, it would have been a simple maneuver to head west, back to Fort Lauderdale. But everything was *not* normal, and all the pilots were having the same problem as Taylor. All the radio controllers who talked to Flight 19 advised them to fly west, but it seemed beyond their comprehension. Radio reception was sketchy, which added to the confusing scenario. None of them even used their ZBX, an instrument that would have guided them back to the base.

A lost pilot, especially a group of lost pilots, who were running low on fuel, would tend to search for the islands that they had passed over within the past hour and a half. Flight 19 made no such effort. Instead, Taylor led the fleet of planes out to open sea in stormy weather. They headed north, then east, then west, then east again. But they never turned back to the islands, where they could've ditched safely near shore.

Instead, they flew on into oblivion, into history, into the lore of the Bermuda Triangle.

Beyond Strange

I want to add two stories as a postscript to the tragic tale of Flight 19. Both show that when it comes to matters of the Bermuda Triangle we are dealing with more than an ordinary mystery. There's an element of the metaphysical trickster at play—the alchemist, the magician, who creates illusions and dabbles with our sense of reality.

The first story dates back to 1991 when, for a brief period of time, it was thought the mystery of Flight 19 had finally been resolved. Five Avenger airplanes from the 1940s were discovered in close proximity in the Atlantic Ocean 10 miles northeast of Fort Lauderdale.

However, deep-sea explorers who investigated the ditched planes from their vessel, *Deep See*, reported that the numbers and markings on the five aircraft differed from the legendary Flight 19. Salvagers and archaeologists speculated that the planes probably crashed in the early 1940s during low-altitude practice torpedo missions.

Graham Hawkes, the lead investigator, noted the irony that there were five planes like Flight 19, and they were the same type of aircraft. "For those who really want to weave a mystery: Instead of one group of five Avengers down in the Bermuda Triangle, we've now given you two, which can only be a good thing, if you like that sort of stuff," Hawkes told the *Miami Herald* in an article on June 5, 1991.

But Hawkes wasn't so cavalier when they first discovered the planes were not Flight 19. He didn't want to believe it. He was certain that these five Avengers must be the remains of the famed flight. The mystery deepened when he discovered that there was no record of these lost planes. If the planes crashed, there certainly would've been a record of the deaths of the pilots. Even if they were ditched by an aircraft carrier, that information would be recorded in the ship's log. No such record has ever materialized.

The planes were discovered while the *Deep See* was searching for a Spanish galleon. "It's like a cruel joke," said Robert Cervoni, managing director of Scientific Search Project of New York, which invested about $50,000 in the find.

He couldn't have said it better. That's the trickster element of the Bermuda Triangle.

The second story might be even stranger.

In June 2016, I received an email from astrologer Ken Hopkins about something curious he had discovered in his research on Flight 19 and the number 23. Because I'm not an astrologer, I forwarded the email to Rob and asked him to show it to his wife, Trish, who has written a number of books on astrology. They met Ken for lunch several weeks later in Cassadaga, Florida, near where he lives, and he brought along a packet of astrological material.

Ken uses declination in his astrological work, which extends the Earth's equator out into space and shows the latitude of the planets in the solar system rather than the longitude. Most Western astrologers use both. In his research with declination, Ken has found that 23 degrees is quite powerful. It is prominent in the charts of many mass events in recent years: the Nice attack, 9/11, and the massacre at Pulse night club in Orlando, and prominent at the moment that Donald Trump entered the 2016 presidential race.

In terms of Flight 19, Ken researched declinations for the 2:10 p.m. departure of the flight from Fort Lauderdale on December 5, 1945; declinations for the natal charts of three of the pilots; declinations for the 7:30 p.m. departure of the rescue flight; and declinations for my natal chart. In all of them, 23 degrees is prominent. It is also prominent for the February 1964 article in *Argosy Magazine* that first labeled the Bermuda Triangle area.

Interestingly, 23 degrees was prominent in other famous disappearances as well, such as the *USS Cyclops* that disappeared sometime after it was last seen in Barbados on March 4, 1918, and the Super Constellation on October 30, 1954. Before we go into what all of this might mean, let's take a look at the rich lore that surrounds the number 23.

In Tangiers in the early 1960s, William Burroughs, author of *Naked Lunch,* knew a Captain Clark who ran a ferry from Tangiers to Spain. Clark boasted that he had been running the ferry for *23 years* without incident. That same day, the ferry sank, killing Clark and everyone on board. That very evening, Burroughs was thinking about this gruesome event, and turned on the radio and heard about the crash of an airplane flying from New York to Miami. The plane was piloted by a *Captain Clark*. It was *flight 23.*

The synchronicity apparently shocked Burroughs enough that he started compiling a list of synchronicities involving the number 23. In 1965, his friend and fellow author Robert Anton Wilson also began putting together a list of oddities about that number. One of the personal synchronicities he noted concerned his daughters. They were born on August *23* and February *23.* Wilson wrote about the number for the *Fortean Times* in 1977. His article appeared in issue number *23.*

In the science and math fields, 23 is also prominent:

- During conception, each parent contributes 23 chromosomes to the fetus.
- Euclid's geometry has 23 axioms.
- The number 23 is the first prime number in which both digits are prime numbers and add up to another prime number.
- It takes 23 seconds for blood to circulate through the human body.
- Every 23rd wave that slams into a shore is twice as large as the average wave.

- The first lunar landing was in the Sea of Tranquility, 23.63 degrees East. The second lunar landing was in the Ocean of Storms, 23.42 degrees West. The first two landings were Apollo 11 and Apollo 12 (11 + 12 = 23).
- The earth rotates completely every 23 hours, 56 minutes.
- The axis of the plane Earth is 23.5 degrees.
- The human biorhythm cycle is 23 days.
  The pattern of DNA shows irregular connections at every 23rd section.
- Humans have 23 vertebra running down the main part of their spines.
- The Harmonic Convergence occurs every 23,000 years.
- Geosynchronous orbit occurs at 23,000 miles above Earth's surface.
- September 23rd is the autumn equinox.
- Since W is the 23rd letter of the alphabet, WWW (for World Wide Web) is 23 + 23 + 23.
- September 11, 2001: 9-11-2001 = 9 + 11 + 2 + 0 + 0 + 1 = 23.

Hollywood also has its own lore about the number 23, for example, the TV show *The X-Files*. The production company, Ten-Thirteen—10 + 13—adds up to 23. The birthdate for Chris Carter, the creator of X-Files, is October 13th (10 + 13 = 23). There is an episode in which an abandoned nuclear silo held a UFO. The number on the silo is 1013. In another episode, Mulder goes to the apartment of a recently deceased man and the number 23 is on the door.

In the popular TV series *Lost*, which builds on layers of synchronicity, there are a number of oddities involving 23:

- Oceanic Flight 815 (8 + 15 = 23).
- The gate number from which the flight departed was 23.
- Jack's seat on the flight was 23A.
- Rose and Bernard were sitting in row 23.

- Hurley stayed in a Sydney hotel on floor 23.
- The reward for turning Kate in was $23,000.
- The number 23 is in the sequence of six numbers that won Hurley the lottery and opened the hatch (4 8 15 16 23 42).

In 2007, a Jim Carrey movie called *The Number 23* met with luke-warm reviews, but the premise is intriguing. Walter Sparrow, an amiable dogcatcher, becomes obsessed with a murder mystery novel that continually circles the number 23. The characters in the novel who become obsessed with the number invariably end up dead. Carrey's character believes the number parallels his own life and that the author is writing about him.

But perhaps the most interesting and revealing instance of the number 23 as it pertains to Flight 19's declinations is found in *The I Ching,* an ancient Chinese divination system based on 64 hexagrams. The 23rd hexagram is called *Splitting Apart.* The gist of it is about disintegration, adversity, and collapse.

Now apply this to Flight 19, a squadron of five planes that vanished in the Bermuda Triangle on December 5, 1945, during a training flight. Apply it to Nice, where a deranged man drove a semi-truck through a crowd and killed 84 people. Or apply it to the September 11th terrorist attacks.

The interpretation of this pattern of 23 depends on which planets are involved. In the declination chart for Flight 19, 23 degrees appears twice in both the northern and southern declination—at the Midheaven/ Pluto and at the North/South Nodes.

In astrology, the Midheaven represents your public persona and Pluto symbolizes profound and irrevocable transformation. The disappearance of Flight 19 has been written about, discussed, dissected, and puzzled over for more than *70* years—not in secret back rooms, but publicly. And with Pluto in the equation, well, no transformation is more profound and irrevocable than death.

The North and South Nodes are often involved in world events and when found in the same degree as other planets or points in a chart, they can point to catastrophe, conflict, and downfall. The 23 degrees for the nodes in the declination chart for Flight 19 happens only every nine years.

As Ken Hopkins concluded in his email to me, "When planets in northern and southern declinations are at the same degree, they may well have an electromagnetic effect on atmosphere."

Ken's idea, of course, is outside of mainstream science. But given what I experienced on my flight—loss of instruments, the electronic fog, weightlessness, and teleportation—Ken's conclusion makes sense to me.

Chapter
5

Dragon's Triangle

Ma-No Umi

Off the coast of Japan in the Western Pacific lies a notorious region of dangerous *Ma-No Umi* waters. The Japanese have known about *Ma-No Umi*—Sea of the Devil—for more than a thousand years. It is now better known as the Dragon's Triangle.

Often compared to the Bermuda Triangle, it is a place where compasses sometimes spin or deviate from true north, radio communications breaks up or go dead, and electronic equipment fails. Huge waves appear along with eruptions of underwater earthquakes (called seaquakes). Intense electrical storms and whirlpools wreak havoc in these historically perilous waters. The sudden appearance of localized fog and bumps in the space-time continuum is said to sometimes alter ships and aircrafts miles from their previous positions. Sightings of ghost ships and UFOs add to the strangeness of this lesser-known triangle, sometimes called a "vile vortex."

Like the Bermuda Triangle, *Ma-No Umi* has claimed countless ships and planes, and usually no trace of the crafts were found. In the past 50 years, more than 3,000 ships and 100 airplanes have disappeared in the Bermuda Triangle, according to a Travel Channel documentary from 2002 called *World of Mysteries: Bermuda Triangle:*

Lost at Sea. Interestingly, the Dragon's Triangle is located at the same geographic coordinates, exactly on the opposite sides of the planet. The Dragon Triangle is also home to the deepest trenches in the world, some descending more than six miles.

Bounded by the central coast of Japan, Manila, and Guam, the *Ma-No Umi* claimed sailing vessels and fishing boats in the distant past when maps indicated that it was a region inhabited by dragons. Ships and planes continued to disappear in the Dragon's Triangle long after belief in dragons faded. Although many wartime disappearances were no doubt related to enemy fire, there still were puzzling incidents that did not seem to involve enemy attacks.

In a case described by Charles Berlitz in *The Dragon's Triangle*, five Japanese warships simultaneously disappeared in maneuvers close to the coast of Japan in early 1942. They included three destroyers and two small aircraft carriers. The case sounds like a parallel to Flight 19 with notable exceptions. Berlitz writes in *The Dragon's Triangle* that the cause of the disappearance of the ships was never ascertained.

It is extremely doubtful that they were sunk by enemy action, since they were in home waters and neither the United States nor Great Britain had, during those dark early days of the war, ships or submarines in the area. Colonel Jimmy Doolittle's bombing raid on Tokyo was months away, as was the Battle of Midway, where the Japanese fleet sustained its first heavy losses. In any case, the Allies would assuredly have quickly taken credit for any sinkings if their forces had been involved.

However, Berlitz doesn't provide the names of any of the ships or a source for the information. Seemingly, the disappearance of five warships in the same waters at the same time would be a well-known story. But that doesn't seem to be the case, which opens up questions about whether the event actually occurred. Berlitz goes on to document numerous other ships that sank in the Dragon's Triangle as well as aircraft that vanished, but the five warships are never mentioned again. In his book *The Bermuda Triangle Mystery Solved* Larry Kusche claimed that the reason the warships weren't named is that they were actually fishing vessels. Of course, if that is true it leaves the question of why five fishing vessels simultaneously vanished.

Probably the best-known story of a ship disappearing involved a research vessel, the *Kaio Maru No. 5*, that was sent out in 1952 by the Japanese government to investigate what was causing the disappearance of ships in those troubled waters. Two years earlier, Japanese officials declared the triangle a danger zone for shipping. The *Kaio Maru* might have found the answer—or one answer—because it vanished with a crew of 31, including nine researchers. No mayday message was sent out and the only wreckage found was five empty oil barrels.

Possible explanations for the disappearance of the ship included the eruption of a seaquake below the vessel, a torpedo from a Russian sub, and a collision with a U.S. naval craft.

In researching the Dragon's Triangle, I came across a skeptic's site called *Skeptoid.* It cited a 2012 article written by Brian Dunning in which he said he was unable to find any historical information related to the Dragon's Triangle. He went on to suggest that it was a made-up phenomenon. "A search for books, newspaper, or magazine articles on the Devil's Sea comes up completely empty, until a full 20 years after the loss of the *Kaio Maru.* Apparently, the story—even the very existence of this legendary named region—was not invented until very recently."

Although Western documentation of this area began with Berlitz's book *The Dragon's Triangle*, published in Great Britain in 1990, the Japanese have feared this region of the sea for centuries. Apparently Dunning didn't research the name *Ma-No Umi*, the Japanese term for the Devil's Sea. If he had, he would have found that the region was long considered perilous waters, the home of dragons.

Into the Past

For more than a thousand years, possibly longer, the Japanese and their neighbors have recorded strange occurrences and disappearances at sea. Ancient records attest to a great slumbering dragon residing in a cavern beneath the sea, and restless dragons surfacing from the depths to drag seamen to their underwater lairs.

The name "Dragon's Triangle" is derived from ancient Chinese fables about underwater dragons that dragged vessels beneath the surface and devoured the seamen. Although he didn't encounter any dragons, the Mongolian emperor Kublai Khan twice experienced the wrath of the Dragon's Triangle when he invaded Japan. In 1274, he amassed a fleet of 900 ships with 40,000 men. A typhoon ripped across the *Ma-No Umi*, sinking more than half of the massive fleet. Undeterred, the Mongolian emperor returned in 1281, this time with 3,000 ships and 140,000 troops. Khan's army stormed the Japanese coast, just as his grandfather Genghis Khan, the Mongol conqueror, had swept across Asia. However, Japan's secret ally, the *kami-kaze*, or divine wind—another powerful typhoon—scattered and sank most of Khan's fleet again. Khan withdrew in defeat and never returned. The Japanese felt protected from invasion by the gods who invoked the *kami-kaze*.

In 1803, Japanese villagers were astonished when a spherical object washed ashore in the Hitachi province on the eastern coast with a mysterious woman inside. The craft featured metallic plates and glass windows. The story became known as *Utsuro-bune*, or "hollow ship," and was recounted in three texts: *Toen shōsetsu* (1825), *Hyōryū kishū* (1835), and *Ume-no-chiri* (1844).

According to the legend, the strange craft was dragged into a village after it was found on the beach. The woman inside looked nothing like the locals: She had white skin, red and white hair, spoke a strange language, and held a rectangular wood box close to her at all times. The "boat" has strange symbols upon it, like nothing the local people had ever seen.

The legend became a cover story, "The Female Alien in a Hollow Vessel," for *Fortean Times* in 1987, when the journal that focuses on scientific anomalies described it as an example of an early alien encounter. Author Masaru Mori noted the similarities of the drawings of the vessel with descriptions of UFOs. He also pointed out that the mysterious symbols on the craft were similar to symbols described by U.S. soldiers who reportedly witnessed a UFO during the famed Rendlesham Forest Incident in England in December 1980. The *Fortean Times* article suggested that the craft might have been an unidentified submerged object (USO) because at least one version of the legend says the craft rose from the depths of the sea.

Japanese scholars who have studied the legend offer another perspective. Kazuo Tanaka, an engineering professor at Gifu University, compared the story to traditional Japanese folklore. Writing in *The Skeptical Inquirer*, he also noted that in the early 19th century Japan was isolated and the appearance of a foreigner in a craft would be a startling incident. He suggested that the woman was British or Russian and that the "unknown writings" on her craft may have been Latin alphabetical characters. However, that explanation ignores the strange shape of the vessel, which was nothing like any European crafts of that time.

Clearly, the Dragon's Triangle has outlived the legend of dragons of the deep. One possible explanation for the long-held belief in deep-sea dragons might be the presence of submarine volcanoes—underwater vents or fissures in the Earth's surface from which magma can erupt. Numerous submarine volcanoes are located near areas of tectonic plate movement, including the Dragon's Triangle.

But volcanoes probably don't account for missing airplanes.

Lost Aircraft

In early 1945, a Japanese Kawanishi Flying Boat on patrol near Iwo Jima vanished. Nothing unusual about that. Japan lost hundreds of aircraft during the war. But on this particular night, prior to the invasion of Iwo Jima, the pilot was expected to report any American aircraft active in the area. No American aircrafts were spotted, but the pilot saw something else. Before disappearing, he made a baffling comment to Shiro Kawamoto, commander of a Zero fighter plane. In an article titled "The Deadly Mystery of Japan's Bermuda Triangle," Rufus Drake quotes Kawamoto, who years later recalled the pilot's last radio transmission. The pilot, who sounded confused, said: "Something is happening in the sky...the sky is opening up." Nothing further was heard and the craft vanished.

In the mid-1950s, long after the war, planes and ships were still disappearing. They include military planes and planes searching for missing cargo ships. Some of the missing planes didn't report any mechanical malfunctions or inclement weather. Berlitz described several cases in his book *The Devil's Triangle* in a chapter entitled "Planes that Never Landed."

A KB-50 with a crew of eight disappeared on March 12, 1957, in good weather on a flight between Japan and Wake Island. There was no SOS and searchers found no trace of the plane or its crew. On March 16, 1957, a U.S. Navy JD-1 Invader disappeared on a routine flight between Japan and Okinawa. Weather conditions were normal and no distress call was received. An extensive search was carried out, but no crew members or wreckage was found.

On March 22, 1957, a C-97 U.S. military transport with 67 personnel aboard disappeared southeast of Japan while beginning its landing approach. The last radio message was sent when the aircraft was 200 miles from Tokyo. No problems were reported. Flying conditions were good. The transport never arrived. A nine-day search and rescue mission covered thousands of square miles of ocean. No trace of the C-97 or its passengers were found.

Those three disappearances of aircrafts near Japan all took place within a nine-day period in 1957 and 80 passengers lost their lives.

Berlitz called it "the nightmare month of aviation." During that same nine-day period, south of the Dragon's Triangle, the president of the Philippines and 24 staff members and crew disappeared on March 19th on a flight near Cebu.

Several other aircrafts were lost in the second half of the 20th century, including KAL Flight 007. On September 1, 1983, the a Korean Air flight left New York City with 269 passengers and flew to Anchorage, then headed for Seoul. However, en route, it strayed into Soviet Union air space and was shot down. The Soviets at first denied knowledge of the attack, then admitted a Soviet Su-15 interceptor shot the commercial airliner near Moneron Island west of Sakhalin in the Sea of Japan. The Soviets justified the attack claiming the plane was on a spy mission. It's unlikely that the Russian pilot who shot down the plane knew its flight number. But the number 007, best known as the code name for the fictional British spy James Bond, was no doubt the only thing about the flight that was related to spying.

Berlitz, for his part, wondered in *The Dragon's Triangle* if the reason the flight crossed into Soviet territory was related to compass malfunctioning.

> It is well known that compasses in certain areas are affected by isogonic force lines between the poles, so that pilots must adjust their compass readings to establish true north and south along the course they are flying.... It is possible that the tragedy of KAL 007 was caused by a temporary magnetic shift, noticed by many pilots in both triangles.

Amelia Earhart

Probably the most famous case of a lost aircraft in the Dragon's Triangle was Amelia Earhart's daring attempt to fly around the world.

Her famed flight was cut short when her Lockheed Electra disappeared over the Dragon's Triangle on June 2, 1937. Earhart and her copilot, Fred Noonan, took off from Lae in Papua New Guinea. Their goal was to reach Howland Island, a distance of about 2,500 miles. Barely 800 miles into the flight, with no warning, her plane vanished.

Within hours, rescue workers began scouring the area for signs of the two pilots. The U.S. Navy and Coast Guard launched the largest and most expensive air and sea search in American history. When their efforts failed, Earhart's husband of six years, George Putnam, financed his own search. When he too came up empty-handed, it was clear that a living legend had vanished into thin air.

Many explanations have been proffered for Earhart's and Noonan's disappearance, ranging form navigational error resulting in the plane running out of fuel and ditching into the ocean or crash-landing on a desert island to the pair being captured by Japanese soldiers and possibly killed or imprisoned for espionage. Even abduction by space aliens has been suggested. Whatever the cause, her tragic ending is forever linked to the Dragon's Triangle.

In an official report, the U.S. government concluded that the two seasoned pilots were unable to locate their destination, ran out of fuel, and crashed into the water and sank. Earhart was declared legally dead on January 5, 1939. The reason for her disappearance remains a mystery.

The espionage theory suggests that Earhart was actually a secret agent working for the U.S. government. She had a close friendship with Franklin D. Roosevelt and his wife, Eleanor. Supporters of that theory suggest that the plane crashed after its pilots intentionally deviated from their course to spy on Japanese-occupied islands in the Pacific, or that Earhart and Noonan landed on one of them and were taken as prisoners.

It could be that Earhart and Noonan entered a fog and found themselves far off course, just as Charles Lindbergh recalled in his autobiography when he wrote about a flight through the Bermuda Triangle.

Space-Time Warps

In the late 1950s, American entertainer Arthur Godfrey was flying over the Dragon's Triangle on an around-the-world tour in his twin-engine jet when, east of Japan, he encountered electronic malfunctions that led to a surprising resolution. Charles Berlitz details this in *The Dragon's Triangle*:

> His flight instruments, including the compasses, the gas gauge, and even the radio, abruptly went dead. With gas for only three hours of flight on hand, Godfrey navigated as well as he could by the sun. After an hour, the instruments suddenly began to operate again, as inexplicable as they had stopped. Godfrey not only found that he was not far off course, but comparing watch time with radio time, he had lost half an hour.

Lieutenant Colonel Frank Hopkins, an advisor to the 106th Air Transport Group, was flying in a C-97 Stratofreighter over the Dragon's Triangle in 1968 when he apparently experienced a breach in the fabric of time and space. He was on a flight from Kwajalein Island to Guam and was a navigator when the incident occurred. As protocol required, he used star navigation to plot their course every hour. Four hours into the flight, he took another celestial fix and was astonished to find that their position was more than 340 nautical miles beyond where they should be.

In *Unearthly Disclosure*, Timothy Good cites Hopkins' description:

> Fourth hour out...I was using good Loran (long-range navigation) and shooting celestial. Ground speed was down to about 230 from the previous fix. Some slight left drift. No problems. Except for the fact that, in ostensibly good weather, a plugging old '97, had, in fact, covered 340 nautical miles in one hour of time for no apparent reason.

When he arrived in Guam, he was told that he wasn't the only pilot who had experienced such displacement. Writes Good: "The head of the weather section informed him that he was aware of such inexplicable phenomenon: it always occurred at night, perhaps eight to ten times a year and lasted not more than two hours."

Hopkins, who died in 2008 at the age of 82, wrote his own obituary. Although he didn't mention his experience, he made one comment that suggested that he never forgot about it. He wrote that his "hobbies were patting dogs, looking at clouds and doing powerful thinking while watching candles burn."

A year prior, in 1967, a missing ship off the coast of Sasebo, Japan, may have been teleported hundreds of miles before sinking, Berlitz contended in *The Dragon's Triangle*. Tokyo Marine Radio received a distress signal from the *Cleveland*, a tanker of 10,265 tons, owned by Cleveland Transport Company of New York. The call for help said there was a fire in the engine room, followed by an urgent message that they were taking on water and abandoning ship. An air-sea search was immediately started and an oil slick was found off Sasebo, which coincided with the approximate position the *Cleveland* had reported. Sasebo is located on the western coast of Kyushu, Japan's southernmost island. When no more remains of the ship or crew were found, the Japanese Maritime Safety Agency advised Cleveland Transport that their ship was lost.

Surprisingly, according to Berlitz's book, Cleveland Transport denied that they had lost the ship, and responded that the *Cleveland* was 3,600 miles away in Bombay (Mumbai). But when the anchorage in Jawaharlal Nehru Port was checked, the ship was no longer there. According to the date that she left the port, it would have been impossible for the ship to sail anywhere near waters off Sasebo at the time of the call for help. The ship would have had to travel at a speed of 120 knots, the land equivalent of 140 miles per hour. That's about six times the normal speed of a tanker.

An article about the missing ship appeared in the *Chicago Tribune* on November 27, 1967. The article's headline read: "Fear U.S. Tanker Sinks Near Japan." Its dateline was "Sasebo, Japan, Nov. 27." The lead sentence read: "SOS messages from an American oil tanker before dawn today said the vessel was afire...and that the 37-man crew was abandoning ship."

The article went on to say that planes from the U.S. Air Force base at Hachikawa joined Japanese aircraft in the search after daybreak. Two U.S. Navy minesweepers and a salvage ship crisscrossed the area along with Japanese patrol boats. A company spokesman denied that the ship was a military troop carrier as previously reported. No mention was made in the article about the disputed location of the ship. However, Berlitz wrote that it was after the search ended when the company denied their ship had sunk because it was in Bombay.

There are numerous reasons that ships sink and planes crash over the Dragon's Triangle. Powerful electrical storms and typhoons, eruptions of underwater volcanoes, seismic sea waves, and tsunamis account for many of the lost crafts. Although there are many explanations, the enduring mystery lies in the cases of apparent teleportation and time travel.

Ghost Ships

Ghost ships come in two varieties: Adrift with no crews, derelicts are spooky, but physical. Even more mysterious are the phantasms—nebulous crafts that were lost at sea, but continue to appear and disappear in their ghostly forms.

In January 1989, a Japanese whaling ship came upon a fishing vessel that was moving erratically and threatened to collide with the ship. The boat was boarded and no crew was found except for the desiccated body of the captain, who was tied to the helm. He apparently had been dead for weeks. No crew members were found. However, a cutlass protruded from his rib cage, no doubt the cause of his death. The scabbard of the cutlass lay nearby on the deck and a single word, written in blood, said: "DEPTHS."

The best known of the paranormal brand of ghost ships is the *Flying Dutchman*, which made a notable appearance in the Dragon's Triangle in 1881. The story of the ship exists somewhere between legend and reality.

Supposedly, the *Flying Dutchman* was a vessel out of Amsterdam that was captained by Hendrick van der Decken—the Dutchman. The ship was making its way toward the East Indies in 1641 when it encountered dangerous weather near the Cape of Good Hope. Determined to make the crossing, van der Decken supposedly went mad, murdered his first mate, and vowed that he would cross the Cape and challenge God's storm. As it is heard in Richard Wagner's opera The Legend of the *Flying Dutchman*, "May I be eternally damned if I do, though I should beat about here till the day of judgment."

Despite his best efforts, the ship sank in the storm, and as the story goes, van der Decken and his ghost ship are now cursed to sail the oceans for all eternity. To this day, the Flying Dutchman continues to be one of the most-sighted of all ghost ships. People from deep-sea fishermen to the Prince of Wales have claimed they glimpsed the phantasmic ship on its never-ending voyage.

The Flying Dutchman has inspired numerous paintings, horror stories, films, and Wagner's 1843 opera. The ship was first mentioned in George Barrington's seafaring book *Voyage to Botany Bay*, published in 1795. Barrington wrote:

In the night watch some of the people saw, or imagined they saw, a vessel standing for them under a press of sail, as though she would run them down: one in particular affirmed it was the ship that had foundered in the former gale, and that it must certainly be her, or the apparition of her; but on its clearing up, the object, a dark thick cloud, disappeared. Nothing could do away the idea of this phenomenon on the minds of the sailors; and, on their relating the circumstances when they arrived in port, the story spread like wild-fire, and the supposed phantom was called the *Flying Dutchman.* From the Dutch the English seamen got the infatuation, and there are very few Indiamen, but what has some one on board, who pretends to have seen the apparition.

Since then its legend has continued to grow, thanks to numerous sightings by fisherman and sailors. One of the most noted sightings occurred deep within the Devil's Triangle when, on the morning of June 11, 1881, the *HMS Bacchante*, a British warship, encountered the legendary *Flying Dutchman*. A young ensign, who would later be crowned King George V, was on a three-year voyage during his late adolescence with his elder brother Prince Albert Victor of Wales and their tutor John Neill Dalton. In *King George V*, Kenneth Rose notes that after the sighting, George wrote in the ship's log:

The Flying Dutchman crossed our bows. She emitted a strange, phosphorescent light as of a phantom ship, all aglow. She came up on the port bow, where also the officer of the watch from the bridge saw her. But on arriving, there was no vestige or any sign whatever of any material ship to be seen, either near of right away to the horizon, the night being clear and the sea calm.

Berlitz was somewhat skeptical about *The Flying Dutchman* and ghost ships in general. Writing in the *Dragon's Triangle*:

Once the legend, especially such a vivid one as the *Flying Dutchman,* becomes established in the consciousness of seafarers, it becomes relatively easy to convince oneself and others that the shape of the legendary ship has come into view. Especially so if, after such a sighting, a seaman is killed in an accident or disappears for some other reason, such as falling into the sea.

Besides ghost ships, ghosts of mariners past supposedly appear on decks of vessels plying the waters of the Dragon's Triangle. One such specter is known as the Chinless Officer, a second mate who appears on the bridge of merchant ships during night watch. He checks the course and asks about weather conditions. Usually, the lower face is covered by a muffler and crew members assume it's a duty officer. But then the muffler falls away, leaving the helmsman gobsmacked as the apparition fades away.

The Chinless Officer, as the story goes, lost his jaw when a steel hook dangling on a crane crashed into his face as it swung above the deck. He died from the injury and has haunted merchant vessels ever since.

UFOs

In ancient times, dragons and demons were considered a serious threat to those who venture onto the high seas off the coast of Japan. On September 24, 1235, strange lights were seen hovering over an army camp in Kyoto. The troops were terrified, thinking the lights were sea dragons coming to attack them.

Now UFOs and unidentified submerged objects (USOs) have replaced dragons by researchers seeking answers beyond mundane meteorological and mechanical explanations for mysterious happenings. The name in Japanese for unidentified flying objects is *Mikakunin Hiko-Buttai*. However, in recent decades *UFO* is the more accepted term.

During World War II, the foo-fighter phenomenon was well known in the European Theatre, but the small metallic-appearing objects also trailed Japanese and American fighter jets over the Dragon's Triangle. They would often appear in clusters—though sometimes as single objects—and were said to emit a steady glow of red, gold, or white light, or they would blink. The name *foo-fighter* supposedly derived from the Smokey Stover comic strip, where it was often said: "Where there's foo there's fire." It may also have been a play on *feu*, the French word for "fire."

The first reported description of foo fighters came from a B-29 bomber, part of the 415th Night Fighter Squadron based at Djon, France. The crew, including Lt. Fred Ringwald, were on a mission to seek out German planes on either side of the Rhine when Ringwald spotted what appeared to be stars in the distance. Within a few minutes, the stars became fast-moving orange balls of light. Though some observers said they appeared metallic, the objects couldn't be picked up by radar. Ringwald said that after following them for a time, the lights disappeared, reappeared farther off, then vanished.

The reports from along the bombing routes to Japan were similar in appearance and actions to those seen in Europe. The speeds were estimated between 200 and 500 miles per hour. U.S. military authorities reported they were a German invention, called *feuerballs*, aimed to confuse radar. Supposedly, documents were found after the war describing the fireballs. If that's the case, then apparently some German and Japanese pilots weren't in the loop because they thought the same objects were secret American weapons pursuing their crafts.

The objects disappeared after the war. No actual foo fighters or even remnants of the secret weapon were ever found, which is surprising since there were so many in the air. The fact that the objects pursued fighter jets over the Pacific raises two questions: 1) How did the Germans control them from such a distance? 2) How were they able to achieve altitudes between 10,000 and 25,000 feet?

Another theory is that the foo fighters were a type of plasma, an electrical discharge (known as St. Elmo's fire), or ball lightening. Whatever they were, the objects seemed to attach to the crafts, while remaining a few hundred feet away, and closely followed the flight paths of their targets. No foo fighters were ever shot down. There are no foo fighters in any World War II museum. What they were remains a mystery.

In an episode of the History Channel's *UFO Files* called "Pacific Bermuda Triangle," Russian researcher Vladimir Ajaja says that UFOs and USOs haunted the former Soviet Union's fleets in the Pacific in the latter decades of the 20th century. According to Ajaja, in 1977 the Soviet Navy ordered a study to examine reports of unidentified objects seen at sea. He was in charge of that group and, by the end of that year, instructions had been given to Soviet naval vessels about how to observe UFOs and what to do when one was spotted.

On August 18, 1980, the *Vladimir Volbirov*, a Soviet research ship, was moving south through the Dragon's Sea on a course toward the Japanese island of Okinawa. Around midnight, a glowing, cylindrical object rose from the sea, hovered, then shot across the sky.

According to the *UFO Files* episode, in 1990, on a quiet beach about 30 miles south of Tokyo, magazine editor Masanobu Miyoshi witnessed a white light "buzzing" a jet that was flying over the ocean. He describes the UFO as moving like it was writing a "W" in the sky. Before his sighting, he did not believe in UFOs, but what he saw has changed his opinion.

On April 17, 1981, the Japanese freighter *Taki Kyoto Maru* was in almost the exact location of the *Vladimir Volbirov* off the east coast of Japan when suddenly the ship was rocked by shockwaves erupting from the sea. An enormous saucer-shaped object rose out of the water, hovered soundlessly, and circled rapidly over the freighter. The seas were calm; the weather clear. In *The Dragon's Triangle*, Berlitz noted that when Captain Usuda was interviewed by journalists in Kanazawa, he said the craft glowed with a blue light and remained for about 15 minutes before plunging back into the sea, almost swamping the 165-foot freighter.

Usuda said that when it circled the ship, it moved so fast that it appeared as a blur. It could only be seen clearly when it hovered. Usuda tried to radio for help, but the electronic equipment was jammed. The ship's instruments spun wildly as the saucer circled. The captain estimated that the ship was four to five times larger in diameter than the length of the ship.

When their instruments returned to normal, the captain found that they had lost 15 minutes of time, the same amount of time that the craft had circled and hovered above them.

The case was recounted by Berlitz in *The Dragon's Triangle* and was well documented. Hoshi Isido, a spokesman for the Japanese coast guard, said: "Based on interviews...and the unusual structural damage...we do suspect that they encountered something very unusual.... Officially we are calling it an unidentified object, a simple UFO."

Mainstream science continues to dismiss UFO reports as misidentification of normal objects and for other non-exotic reasons, such as fakery. So it's interesting that in 1988 the Japanese edition of *Scientific American* (*Nikkei Science*) published an article about a Japanese mariner who had witnessed two UFOs. The first incident occurred in 1984 when the Japanese research ship *Kaiyo Maru*—apparently a popular name for Japanese ships—was off the Falkland Islands in the South Atlantic. A crewman, referred to as Mr. Naganobu, saw two dozen UFOs hovering in the sky until they abruptly shot off in three directions. Two years later, Naganobu was aboard the ship in the Dragon's Triangle when a huge, cigar-shaped UFO, more than 100 feet in length, approached the ship and plunged into the ocean. This time the event was also seen on radar.

Finally, here's a tale of a UFO encounter from *above* the Dragon's Triangle that was documented in *UFO Sightings UFO Files: The Pacific Bermuda Triangle*. On March 18, 1965, the captain of a Japanese Toa Airways Convair jetliner encountered a large, oblong-shaped craft. To avoid a collision, he turned 60 degrees at more than 500 miles per hour. The UFO, according to Berlitz's account, stopped suddenly and then maneuvered alongside the airliner. The captain radioed that he was being shadowed by a UFO.

He described that the object was around 50 feet long and glowed with a greenish hue. A pilot in another aircraft heard the Toa captain's frantic radio transmissions, and the object was independently spotted several times that night at different locations.

Chapter 6

The Power of Electronic Fog

Twenty-five years after my narrow escape from the Bermuda Triangle phenomenon, I encountered the same mysterious fog near the Florida Keys. It seemed that I was flying through an enormous mass of fog that went on mile after mile. But just like the first time, airport traffic controllers were reporting clear skies with no extensive areas of fog. As a result, I discovered something about the nature of this fog that would explain why it didn't show up on radar.

On that day in February 1996, Lynn and I took off from Tavernier in the upper keys, on a flight for West Palm Beach. I called Miami Flight Service for a weather briefing at about 8 a.m. The weather in South Florida was clear, with visibility at around six miles and winds out of the east at 10 miles per hour. A few medium-sized thunderstorms were starting to form over Florida Bay, so we had to get going before the storms reached us.

We waited patiently while our neighbor and friend Carl took off in his Cessna Skymaster. I had no idea that Carl's flight would impact ours. About 15 minutes after he departed, we taxied down the runway. I noticed a thunderstorm just to the west was starting to spread toward us. We needed to quickly get in the air. Light rain from the storm pelted the windshield as we lifted off the runway and climbed over Florida Bay.

Several minutes later, as we flew north toward the Everglades, Carl radioed his location 15 miles north of us and said he was turning back to Tavernier. I thought that was odd because he said he was going to Tampa. I radioed Carl to let him know our position. I had talked to Carl on the radio while flying many times, and I noticed his voice sounded tense. He always liked chatting it up on the radio, but this time he seemed subdued and said very little.

Just before we reached the Everglades I heard Carl talking to another airborne neighbor who asked him why he wasn't going to Tampa. "We had to turn back because the weather is just terrible! It looks like the whole state is socked in with heavy fog."

That puzzled me, because no fog was mentioned in the weather briefing. But I knew fog could form quickly, especially right after sunrise. There are two known types of fog: radiation fog, which is also called ground fog; and advection or sea fog, which forms over bodies of water. Radiation fog appears when cool ground contacts warm air; sea fog forms when moist air moves over colder water. Unlike ground fog, sea fog can move rapidly and form any time of the day. It's usually more extensive and remains longer than radiation fog.

As we continued inland, thick fog surrounded us. Ever since my experience in 1970, fog like this troubled me. I was getting tense. It seemed as though we were flying through radiation fog and I was concerned that we might run out of gas before the fog dissipated. I had two hours of gas left and if I turned back, as Carl had done, Tavernier would probably get pounded by a thunderstorm.

I called the Miami Flight Service for an update on the weather and said I was 10 miles south of Homestead. I was told there was no fog and visibility was six miles. I couldn't believe what I had heard. I still didn't know what to do. I looked north toward Miami, but all I could see was fog. So I asked where the fog ended. The weather briefer responded: "I have no idea what you're looking at. There's no fog anywhere in this area."

Now I was more puzzled than ever. I had a feeling that if I headed toward a large body of water, the fog might dissipate. So I decided to fly out over the ocean to see if we could escape the fog. As we headed east toward the Atlantic, I studied the fog more closely and noticed something odd. There was no fog directly below the plane, and as we continued the opening remained below us. It was like looking down a cylinder. It didn't make sense. How could there be fog all around us, but none below us?

Within minutes we were nearing the ocean and the clear cylinder below us began to expand. I could see the ground we were passing over. That's when I realized that we couldn't get out of the fog because it seemed as though the fog was moving with us at 180 miles an hour.

Then I noticed something else that was just as baffling. As I looked through the expanding opening, I noticed a distinct line separating the fog and the ground. There was a kink in the line, which I focused on. Eventually, the opening expanded all the way to the horizon, but the warped line didn't disappear.

I tried to relax and settle back as I watched one of the most curious meteorological phenomena I had ever witnessed. After another 10 minutes, the kinked segment in the line between the fog and the clear sky began to fade, and the fog started to dissipate. Even after the fog disappeared, I could still see remnants of the kinked line in the distance encircling the airplane like a halo for the rest of the flight, which lasted another 25 minutes. The warped line even remained visible during the final approach to the airport.

I remained puzzled over the nature of that unusual fog until a few years later when I read about another pilot, Martin Caidin, who had experienced it. Outlandish as it sounded, the fog seemed to cling to the airplane like static electricity on clothing. Rather than flying through a massive blanket of fog, a pocket of fog had attached to the plane and was moving along with it. That's why the weather briefer had told us there was no fog on the radar.

Bruce and daughter Keely with the Cessna that Bruce and Lynn Gernon flew during his second encounter with electronic fog.
Photo credit: Lynn Gernon.

Naming the Fog

I'm convinced that many pilots have flown into this unusual fog without realizing it. When a pilot from New Jersey read about my flight in Berlitz's *Without a Trace,* he called me in 1977 and told me about a similar cloud he encountered on a flight in 1952 between the Florida Keys and Vero Beach, Florida.

He was at 7,000 feet, about five miles offshore from Fort Lauderdale on a clear day when his plane suddenly entered a fog or haze. It was like nothing he had ever encountered. It reminded him of static on a television after the cable goes out. He said it was like "electric fog." After he hung up, I thought to myself, *No, electronic fog.* That's how I came up with the name.

Mystery Flight

One of the best documented encounters with electronic fog occurred on June 11, 1986, when a Consolidated PBY-6A Catalina took off from Bermuda en route to Jacksonville. What's particularly significant about this encounter is that several experienced pilots were aboard. They included Captain Art Ward, a U.S. Navy pilot and instrument instructor; Randy Sohn, a jetliner captain from Northwest Airlines; and Major General Malcolm Ryan, a test pilot and combat leader. Also on board were the Catalina's owner Connie Edwards; his wife, Karen; and author Martin Caidin and his wife, Dee Dee. All four were also experienced pilots. Caidin, an author of numerous books, including many on aviation, later wrote about what happened in *Ghosts of the Air: True Stories of Aerial Hauntings.*

Electronic fog attaches to an airplane, moves with it, and often a circular opening in the fog travels with fog and plane.
Art credit: Bruce Gernon.

Caidin described the Catalina as a large flying boat that was out-fitted with state-of-the-art navigational equipment, including two location finders, a radar altimeter, and multiple radios. Their naviga-tion systems would let them know if they were so much as a tenth of a mile off the planned course. They were linked to a weather satellite, which allowed them to print out photographs taken from space show-ing where they were flying at the moment.

When they departed from Bermuda, the weather was clear and calm, and they expected an uneventful flight. Caidin was stand-ing between the two pilot seats, watching dolphins through the side window, when he shifted his gaze from the right side of the plane to the left. One moment he was looking out over the wing, and the next moment the wing vanished into a thick yellow cloud or fog that had risen up to 4,000 feet and engulfed the plane. "Suddenly, with-out a bump or a tremor or any indication that things were different, the outside world was gone," Caidin recalled in his book. "Nothing changed except that the airplane now was flying through a huge mass of yellow eggnog."

With no reference points visible outside of the plane, they needed to rely on their instruments. That's called flying in Instrument Meteorological Conditions (IMC). But when the pilots looked at the instruments they were startled to see that all the gauges were fail-ing. The LORAN, a radio navigation system, was useless, incapable of finding their location or anything else. The needle on the mag-netic compass swung back and forth, then spun in a blur. The gyro-scopic instrument that created an artificial horizon failed. Even the electronic fuel gauges became erratic. "Our intricate navigation gear blinked a few times and then every dial read: 8888888. Then the radio went dead!" Caidin wrote.

In spite of the fog, they were surprised to discover that they could look through tunnels above and below the plane. Looking up through the tunnel, they could see patches of blue sky. Looking down, they could glimpse the ocean. They continued flying in what they hoped was a westerly direction by aiming the plane toward a bright area above the horizon. The only instrument that worked was a turn-slip-skid indicator that "operates like a seal balancing a ball on its nose, and functioned without outside power."

They flew in the fog for more than three hours. During that time, they descended as low as 20 to 30 feet and found that the fog remained with them no matter what. They went up to 8,000 feet and found the same "eggnog." (Altimeters measure altitude through atmospheric pressure and don't require electrical power to function.) About 90 minutes outside of Jacksonville, they suddenly emerged from the yellow sky and into bright, clear air. They looked back and there was no sign of the fog. They took a wide turn for a better view. "The sky was absolutely clear behind us as far as we could see. Whatever had enveloped us for hours was gone."

All the electronic equipment started operating again. With radios working, they contacted Jacksonville Naval Air Station and proceeded to land without any difficulty. They survived an encounter with electronic fog, but only because they were experienced pilots and took turns piloting the plane.

Caidin's conclusions about the flight in *Ghosts of the Air* came close to describing the nature of electronic fog.

> The single explanation that appears to make sense is that the Catalina flying boat was enveloped or affected by an intense electromagnetic field that dumped the instruments and "blanked out" the electronic equipment. . . . Any pilot caught in that "soup" who lacked experienced flying skills with basic instruments and no outside reference would almost certainly have lost control and crashed in the ocean.

I was impressed by the similarities between the Catalina flight and my own experiences regarding electronic fog. In my first flight, my electronic equipment failed. Like Caidin, when I left the fog, it was nowhere to be seen when I looked back. In my second experience, I also noticed the hole in the fog below the plane. It was after reading Caidin's account of his flight that I came to the conclusion that electronic fog attached itself to airplanes. It goes on and on, mile after mile. But as I discovered, it's actually a very localized fog that may radiate out only a quarter of a mile as it clings to the aircraft.

Corroborating Experiences

Those who have escaped encounters with electronic fog are the ones who can testify to its existence and can speak for the many others who entered the fog and lost their lives. Take the case of Cary Trantham, who flew into the fog in 1995 on a flight in the Florida Keys. It was a year before my second flight into the fog and in the same area between Miami and the keys. At the time, Cary was the manager of a flying club at the Boca Chica Key Naval Air Station, had flown the club's Piper Warrior many times, and was familiar with the route.

On the day of her frightening experience in the cockpit, she flew to Ormond Beach in central Florida to visit her daughter. They met at the airport, then went out for lunch and shopping. On her way back to the keys, Cary dodged scattered clouds on her flight south. The sun was about to set as she flew over Tampa–St. Petersburg and, as she neared Naples, she saw the lights of Miami to the east. Overhead, high clouds blocked the moon and stars. Then, as she passed over the Everglades, a haze formed below her.

"Suddenly, it was as if someone threw a blanket over the airplane," she wrote in an article published in the April 2003 issue of *AOPA Pilot*, an aeronautical journal for general aviation. The horizon was gone and she panicked. She didn't know if she was right-side up or upside down.

When she looked at the instruments, her confusion multiplied. The compass was spinning, and the illumination in the cockpit began to fluctuate from dim to bright and back again. The attitude indicator began to roll, and there was a high-pitched buzzing in her headset.

Cary thought about a documentary she had seen about the Bermuda Triangle with its missing airplanes and ships, instrument malfunctions, and magnetic anomalies. She couldn't help wonder if she was going to be the next victim. Terrified, she fought off panic. She tried making radio contact with Miami, but there was no response.

She recalled a conversation with a jet pilot in the Navy Flying Club. He told her that there was dead-air space in an area over the Gulf between the mainland and the keys. Maybe this was what he was talking about, she thought. She shifted frequencies and was relieved to hear the voice of an air traffic controller. But her instruments were still out and a dense darkness surrounded her plane, blocking out any illumination.

About 20 minutes later, she realized that she saw lights on the horizon and was told it was Marathon. She knew she would escape the fog. She followed the string of keys and eventually landed safely back at the naval air station.

"I realized how lucky I was, and how close I came to the 'dead-man's spiral' and being another lost airplane in the Bermuda Triangle." The dead-man's spiral or graveyard spiral is an unintentional maneuver by inexperienced pilots flying in conditions with poor visibility. The pilot experiences spatial disorientation and tends to repeatedly pull back on the yoke to avoid crashing. Eventually, the plane spins into a deadly spiral that is difficult to escape.

"I don't question why I survived," Cary wrote. "For whatever reason, it was a miracle, as all odds were against me." Cary had told her stories on Bermuda Triangle documentaries for the National Geographic Channel, the Learning Channel, the SyFy Channel, and the Discovery Channel. She has also written a book called *Bermuda Triangle: Pathway to Atlantis.*

Unfortunately, not everyone has Cary's luck. Case in point, the next story is one that took place close to where both Cary and I encountered the fog. It involves an experienced pilot who couldn't escape fog shrouding his plane even though other pilots were nearby and reported clear weather. Ironically, the pilot, Casey Purvis, and his copilot, Rob Fuller, were posing as drug runners, attempting to avoid a Coast Guard aircraft patrol.

A Mystery Crash

Casey Purvis was a successful businessman and highly experienced pilot who enjoyed working with the U.S. Coast Guard auxiliary, according to a report by the National Transportation Safety Board—NTSB Identification: MIA01GA070. His last flight was on February 1, 2001, when he encountered a fog, couldn't escape it, and dove into the ocean as a result.

Just before the crash, the lead pilot for the Coast Guard, who was flying a Coast Guard Falcon jet, was moving south over the Everglades at an altitude of 1,000 feet. About half a mile ahead of them, Purvis was flying his Piper Archer 32-300 at 1,500 feet. As the plane approached the ranger station in Flamingo, Purvis was asked if he was comfortable continuing an additional two or three miles. He said that was no problem, and that he could see the Marathon airport about 25 miles to the south.

However, a minute or so later, Purvis reported that he was surrounded by a haze. The Coast Guard plane turned north and the crew asked Purvis to follow at a slower pace so they could get greater distance between them for another intercept. He responded that he was flying by instruments and that he would continue flying in a southerly direction.

The Falcon jet crew informed Purvis that they were well ahead of him in clear weather and there was no conflict with their craft. A short time later they called Purvis again, but this time he didn't answer. Several more calls were made, and when there was no response, a search was launched for the missing pilot.

In spite of the Coast Guard's request to turn north, Purvis continued flying to the south. According to the radar data, the Piper was southbound at 1,600 feet at 7:47 p.m. For the next several minutes, the plane made slight maneuvers to the right, then left, for a total of seven unexplained turns. The plane dropped to 1,500 feet, and then vanished from the radar at 7:51 p.m.

Purvis was an avid volunteer in the auxiliary program and often flew 20 to 30 hours per week for the group. He had a spotless flying record with no accidents, incidents, or violations. He had recorded 1,586 hours of flight time, including 1,375 of them in the Piper. He flew 149 hours at night and 65 hours flying by instruments, and he was instrument rated. He worked with the Coast Guard for more than two years.

When the plane was recovered from six feet of water, NTSB found no evidence of mechanical failure or faulty instruments. The pilot's son reported that the gas tank of the plane had been filled before take-off. Even though Purvis had reported fog and poor visibility, weather conditions at the time were clear, with a visibility of nine miles and light winds.

The NTSB concluded that Purvis had become spatially disoriented, was unable to tell which way was up, and flew into the ocean. The report stated:

> Lack of natural horizon or such reference is common in over-water flights, and especially at night in sparsely populated areas, or in low-visibility conditions. The disoriented pilot may place the aircraft in a dangerous attitude. Therefore, the use of flight instruments is essential to maintain proper attitude when encountering any of the elements, which may result in spatial disorientation.

Yet, as noted, Casey Purvis was experienced at flying in such conditions. He had flown frequently at night and also was comfortable using only instruments. However, if the instruments had temporarily failed as a result of electromagnetic anomalies, that situation would offer a better explanation about why Purvis flew his plane into the sea.

The following two stories about the fog were both seen from the surface of the ocean, rather than from the sky. The first is from a fishing boat, the second from the deck of a Navy ship.

Pursued by Fog

One day while having the upholstery of my single-engine Maule repaired, I began talking with the upholsterer about my experiences with electronic fog. To my surprise, Tony responded with his own story about an encounter with mysterious fog. In Tony's case, the incident took place at sea level while he and a friend were fishing one night in 1992.

The two fishermen were five or six miles off the coast of Palm Beach County when around 1 a.m. they noticed glowing lights on the horizon to the northeast. The lights got brighter, then turned greenish.

"At first, we thought it might be a ship moving our way," Tony recalled. "As it got closer to us, it appeared like a bubble of light."

When it was about a mile away, they saw that it was a luminous bank of fog. It kept coming toward them, and they were getting anxious. They started the engine when it was a couple hundred yards away. "It looked like a translucent green wall. But it wasn't wispy like regular fog. It was flat on top and rounded on the sides and was about 400 to 500 yards across."

To their surprise, the fog seemed to keep pace with them. "It made a beeline right toward us. I turned toward the beach, and we were moving at about 25 to 30 knots."

Finally, when they were about a hundred yards from shore, it began to break apart. "We didn't talk about it afterward. It was just too weird, getting chased for miles by a green bubble of fog."

Tony doesn't know what would have happened if they had been caught by the fog, and at the time he definitely didn't want to find out. "I was just glad to get back to land."

Aboard Ship

David wrote to me in 2013 about his experience after watching *Bermuda Triangle Exposed* on the Discovery Channel.

> I was thrilled to hear about what you experienced. You are not alone, not by far. You may have been the only one to experience the fog in flight, but I was on the USS Harold J Ellison in the 1970s and we went through the Triangle a number of times event free. But the last time, we encountered the fog.

David recalled that it was a beautiful day, and the water was calm and smooth as glass. Then the crew saw a cloud in front of them. "It reached the surface of the water, and as we entered it, you could watch the ship disappear into the fog." Suddenly, they were in heavy seas with huge waves and high winds.

> I was on forward lookout. My post was on top of the pilot house, but because of the weather, I was called down into the pilot house where I was able to watch in safety. We lost radio communications and we also lost both gyro and magnetic compasses, as well as radar.

As if to place an exclamation point on the electromagnetic storm, David said St. Elmo's Fire and balls of lightning bounced all over the ship.

There was a couple of other freaky things, but the weirdest was what happened when we got our Pathfinder Radar back. The radar showed a cloud formation that amazingly spelled the word "HELP." We all saw it. The captain was on deck and asked the officer of the deck if he wanted to report the radar image. He said, "No, who would believe it?" Then the storm ended as suddenly as it had begun. We came out of the fog and the water was again as smooth as glass and the skies were sunny. I remembered all of this because it was so unusual.

He noted that at a reunion of shipmates a couple of years earlier, he found one former sailor who had been aboard during that storm. "I talked to him about it and he remembered it as well. Unlike your story, we didn't have a time disruption or a location displacement. It was just freaky."

Ball Lightning and St. Elmo's Fire

It might seem as though I'm switching subjects from electronic fog, but that's not necessarily the case. All three phenomena—ball lightning, St. Elmo's fire, and electronic fog—are related to electromagnetic storms. Their appearance and behavior have been observed, and yet they remain elusive phenomena. Science, of course, accepts lightning as fact, because it's readily observable, and can even be reproduced to some extent in laboratory conditions. But when observations are infrequent and the observers typically aren't scientists, then acceptance of an unknown phenomenon remains questionable.

Although mysterious luminous balls of energy of various sizes have been seen for centuries, usually in relationship to electrical storms, mainstream science didn't document the existence of ball lightning until January 2014 when Chinese scientists, who were mapping radiation, accidentally recorded ball lightning near a lightning strike. A few months prior, scientists at the U.S. Air Force Academy in Colorado photographed glowing plasmoid balls in their laboratory. The balls were generated from high-power electric sparks, discharged by electrodes partly submerged in electrolyte solutions.

But so little is known about ball lightning that they called it "ball lightning–like atmospheric pressure plasmoids" in an article published in *The Journal of Physical Chemistry.*

Likewise, little is known about St. Elmo's fire, small glowing balls of energy usually related to ships at sea. Sailors have reported it accompanying their ships for centuries, and usually consider it a sign of good luck, as St. Elmo represents an alternate name for St. Erasmus, the patron saint of sailors.

Similarly, electronic fog is related to stormy weather, and like St. Elmo's fire, it travels with the craft. However, from stories I've received it appears that electronic fog has the capacity to last hours past the life of the storm, which is why some of the extraordinary stories of electronic fog seem unrelated to stormy weather.

From my experience, electronic fog formed when I entered the tunnel vortex on my flight. Puffs of clouds hovered a few yards inside the tunnel walls. They were slowly rotating counter-clockwise. When I exited the tunnel, the clear sky I had seen through the tunnel was gone, replaced by the fog, and all of the plane's electronic equipment failed. As I explained, the plane temporarily disappeared from radar, then reappeared 90 miles from our previous location.

Measuring the Fog

Electronic fog, I've realized, reacts to aircraft just as lightning is attracted to the tallest object in its path. It literally hitches a ride on passing crafts. I'm convinced that the fog is responsible for some of the baffling incidents reported by pilots such as Purvis, aeronautics author Martin Caidin, Charles Lindbergh, commercial pilot John Hawke (see Chapter 10), and many others inside and outside the

Bermuda Triangle. But I've found that the intensity of the experiences fluctuate from case to case.

These experiences can vary greatly from a moderately disorienting situation to an extremely dangerous one. Sometimes electronic equipment malfunctions, and that can send pilots to their deaths. In some instances, it even hurtles the craft, pilot, and passengers through a breech in the space-time continuum. That is what I experienced on my flight in 1970.

To that end, I've devised a five-level scale to describe the various stages of electronic fog. I've experienced two of the levels myself during my many flights into the Bermuda Triangle. The following description of the scale is oriented to aircrafts.

The Gernon Scale of Electronic Fog

1. Appears as a mist or haze with visibility of between two and three miles. Magnetic and electronic navigational equipment are not affected, but the fog clings to the plane.
2. Creates the illusion that the fog rises from the surface and spreads out for an unlimited distance below the craft. The sky overhead is clear, and a tunnel or shaft may appear directly below the plane revealing the earth or water. Visibility is near zero within the fog with the exception of the shaft. Magnetic and electronic navigational equipment are not affected.
3. Completely surrounds the aircraft with the exception of two shafts—one above and one below the plane. Visibility is near zero in the fog and unlimited in the shaft. Magnetic and navigational equipment will malfunction, including radios, after a period of time.
4. Surrounds aircraft with visibility severely limited and obscured to shades of gray. Visibility appears to be from one

to two miles. The sun or moon will be not visible, but can be determined by the intensity of brightness. Landmarks may be identified, but will appear hazy. Electronic and navigational equipment will malfunction, but radios will work, at least for the first few minutes. Space-time warps may take effect.

5. Appears to envelop the aircraft with visibility totally obscured. Magnetic and navigational equipment fails, including radios. Space-time warps occur instantaneously upon entry and induce total disintegration of the aircraft and its occupants.

Electronic fog is an outgrowth of powerful electromagnetic storms that materialize suddenly, then disappear. Pilots might enter a Category 1 electronic fog and experience only a haze or mist, nothing

Bruce and Lynn Gernon by their 1991 Beechcraft Bonanza, identical—except more technologically advanced—to his 1970 Bonanza that he flew through the tunnel vortex. Photo credit: Keely Burton.

Two thunderheads coming together. The second photo, taken a minute and a half later, shows a tunnel forming between the two storms. The tunnel is similar to the one Bruce Gernon flew through. However, in his case, there was no other way out. The clouds formed a huge doughnut around him, spanning from the ocean to 50,000 feet. Photo credit: Bruce Gernon.

that seems out of the ordinary. When pilots enter a Category 2 or 3 electronic fog, they probably won't see the mother storm, either. (That was the case with my second encounter described at the beginning of the chapter.)

Whereas pilots caught in a Category 2 or 3 fog see only the haze, the mother storm itself is enormous and short-lived. The storm I experienced in 1970 materialized quickly and expanded to a diameter of 30 miles and rose from the ocean to 40,000 feet within 20 minutes.

I don't know of any other pilot who has experienced this storm from its birth, flown directly through the heart of it, and exited through a tunnel vortex. At that point, I was enveloped in electronic fog of a Category 4 level. If others have duplicated my feat, they probably didn't live to tell about it.

Category 5 electronic fog is not only hypothetical, but virtually impossible to prove. There are no survivors, no documentation. So as a plane flies into Category 5 electronic fog, the pilot literally flies into the mythical Bermuda Triangle—or one of its counterparts—a place that may exist more in the mind than in physical reality.

Electronic fog doesn't only affect airplanes, and it doesn't only appear above water. In the next chapter, we'll explore encounters on land as well as on the water far from the Bermuda Triangle, and in the air over land.

Chapter 7

The Fog Beyond

Through the years, many of the emails I've received were sent by students writing papers on the Bermuda Triangle. Others have come from people who told me about their experiences with mysterious fog. I collected these stories, and noticed that a surprising number of them were about incidents that took place far outside of the Bermuda Triangle. I began to realize I was researching a phenomenon that wasn't solely linked to the waters off the east coast of Florida, north of Bermuda, and south of Puerto Rico.

I already suspected that the Bermuda Triangle wasn't unique. Not only are there other locales where electronic fog appears, such as the Dragon's Triangle and, as you'll read later in this chapter, the Lake Michigan Triangle, but it seems that the fog can manifest virtually anywhere when conditions are right. In the air, on the water, and on land.

The following story is an astonishing account of apparent time travel recounted by British Royal Air Force pilot Sir Victor Goddard in his book, *Flight Toward Reality*. It took place in 1935 on a flight in Scotland, and Goddard never forgot what happened.

Flying Through Time

On a weekend four years prior to when England entered World War II, Wing Commander Victor Goddard flew a Hawker Hart biplane to

Edinburgh from his home base in Andover, England. On Sunday, the day before his return flight, Goddard made a short flight to inspect an abandoned airfield in Drem, about 20 miles from Edinburgh. He found that foliage had overtaken most of the field and cattle roamed about. The tarmac and four hangars were in disrepair. The property was a farm, and the airfield was useless.

The next day, in spite of stormy weather, Goddard took off on his return flight. He followed a route that would lead him over Drem again. But with the low clouds and heavy rain, he didn't expect to see the village or the abandoned airfield. To make matters worse, Goddard was flying in an open cockpit over rugged terrain with no radio navigation support or modern instruments to guide him.

Torrential rain stung his forehead and ran down his goggles. He climbed to 8,000 feet in the hope of flying above the storm, but he couldn't find any break in the dense cloud cover. With no horizon visible, the nose of the biplane dipped too low and he lost control as the plane slipped into a death spiral, falling from the sky. He struggled with the controls, but couldn't pull out of the spin.

The sky darkened, the rain pounded, and the clouds turned yellowish. Goddard was dropping rapidly at 150 miles per hour. His altimeter revealed he was just a thousand feet above the ground, then at 200 feet he glimpsed daylight. He emerged from the clouds still plunging toward water, which he recognized as the Firth of Forth.

Somehow, he managed to pull out of the spin at the last moment. He was flying at 20 feet when he saw a young girl with a baby carriage running through the pouring rain. She ducked to avoid his wing and he barely cleared a stonewall. He flew along the beach, his view obscured by fog. He turned away from the water and glimpsed the black silhouettes of the Drem Airfield hangars ahead of him.

As he recounted in his book, the sky remained dark, the downpour heavy, and his plane began to shake. Still flying several feet above the ground, the hangars loomed in front of him. Suddenly, the rain stopped and the sun was shining brightly. The hangars and airstrip now appeared in new condition, and the cattle were gone. He could see mechanics by four yellow planes near the end of the runway. One of the crafts was a monoplane unlike anything in the Royal Air Force. The airplane mechanics wore blue overalls. But RAF mechanics only wore brown overalls.

He passed over the airport just high enough to clear the hangars, but none of the mechanics reacted, as if they didn't see or hear him. As he left the airfield behind, he was swallowed by the storm again. This time he flew up to 17,000 feet, and briefly up to 21,000 feet to avoid the storm, and made his way safely back to the base.

When he told several officers about his eerie flight, they reacted as if he had lost his mind. So he didn't say anything more, fearing that he would be grounded or discharged from the RAF.

In 1939, Goddard's vision began to materialize as he saw RAF training planes painted yellow, mechanics switching to blue overalls, and a new monoplane—the Magister—just like the one he witnessed four years prior. He also found out that with war about to be declared, the airfield at Drem had been refurbished.

What particularly fascinated me about Goddard was that in the aftermath, he did the same thing I did. He replayed the experience over and over again in his mind for the next 27 years. Finally, in 1966, he wrote about the experience. He had become convinced that there was no way he could possibly have known four years in advance that the color of the trainer planes and the overalls of the mechanics would change. He concluded that he had briefly glimpsed the future or traveled into it just as I concluded years ago that I had instantly leaped ahead 90 miles after flying through the tunnel vortex of the storm.

~~~~~~

In a few of the stories I've received, UFOs seemingly played a role in their mysterious experiences. For years, I tried to avoid the topic, not wanting to sound like a UFO nut when talking about my experiences. However, I have come to realize the subject can't be avoided, that it somehow is a factor in at least some of these mysterious experiences involving breaches in the space-time continuum. The following story is one in which a pilot experienced a shift in space and time after sighting a UFO.

Sudden Darkness

A Colorado pilot wrote to me about a flight that took place in the mid-1970s. Benjamin was flying westward in his Aerona C-150 across La Veta pass in Colorado, a familiar route for him that followed the Combres & Toltec Railroad tracks. The weather was clear and calm. He would be landing in Alamosa within a minute or two of sunset with half an hour of fuel left, about four gallons.

"The checkpoints were clicking off just right. The sun was getting low and I was closing in on my destination. That was when I saw a silver, disk-shaped object hovering about a quarter of a mile away. Then suddenly it was dark."

He spotted an airport beacon ahead and focused on landing. He called the tower, but oddly no one responded. So he landed and was shocked to find that he was at the Perry Stokes Airport in Trinidad about 50 miles west of Alamosa. Probably no one had responded to his call because he was on the frequency for the Alamosa airport. Benjamin checked the time and found that he had been flying slightly more than an hour longer than he expected.

"I should've crashed in the rocks from fuel exhaustion half an hour earlier," he attested. That wasn't his only surprise. The next morning when he re-fueled, he found that he had landed with four gallons of fuel, the same amount he expected to have if he'd landed in Alamosa.

How could Benjamin have flown for an hour without using all of his remaining fuel? And how did he end up at Trinidad? The other factor was the UFO. He had seen it in the waning light of day, then abruptly it was dark and he was 50 miles off course. In addition, an hour had passed. It seems that something very strange had happened in that hour that he wasn't able to remember.

~~~~~

I used to think that electronic fog only occurred over water. But after receiving numerous stories from motorists about their mysterious encounters with fog, I've come to believe that the fog can appear virtually anywhere. Typically, these stories involve a leap in space—motorists arriving too soon at their destinations, as if they were teleported ahead after entering the fog.

Timestorm

About a year after *THE FOG* was published in 2005, I received an email from Don Pilz, a recently retired county sheriff in Indiana. He had just finished the book and wanted to tell me about his own experience that he found eerily similar to mine—except Don was driving a car when he encountered what sounds a lot like electronic fog.

He was taking his elderly father home from a doctor's office around 1 p.m. when he noticed a strange-looking cloud. It seemed to rise directly from the ground like a vertical wall. As they drove toward it, a huge silvery sphere of ball lightning, about 40 feet in diameter, crossed in front of them.

They immediately started to feel nauseous, so Don pulled over to the side of the road. As they watched the sphere move toward the wall of the storm, a tunnel about 100 feet in diameter opened up in the storm and the sphere disappeared into it. At that point, both Don and his father became disoriented, and when he checked the time he was startled to find that it was almost 5 p.m. They had somehow lost more than three hours of time.

Don was obsessed with the event and was determined to find out exactly what happened. I suggested that he try to obtain the radar video images from that time and location. I figured that as a former high-ranking county official, he might gain access to such government material. It took more than a year, but he was finally able to get the radar video, and it was stunning.

It showed five donut-shaped storm rings, similar to the one that had captured my plane, scattered across the state. The ring that Don and his father had encountered formed spontaneously with an outside circumference of about 40 miles and an inside diameter of about 20 miles. The storm completely dissipated after 20 minutes.

I kept in touch with Don for months, and when a Japanese TV station contacted me about plans for a documentary on the Bermuda Triangle, I told them about Don and his research. They interviewed both of us and displayed Don's video of his "timestorm."

After appearing on TV, Don became even more consumed in his research and started working on a book. While I told him I thought the sphere related to electronic fog, he became convinced that it was an alien inter-dimensional craft. Unfortunately, he died in 2010 before he finished his book.

A Jump Ahead

The next story is from a retired Air Force officer who describes a baffling experience that has puzzled him for years. "My experience took place in 1999 or 2000 and after hearing you describe your experience flying through the storm tunnel or time warp, I see a link to my experience. However, this was not in the ocean or in the air, but on the ground," he wrote to me in 2014.

Jonathan explained that he has traveled dozens of times for many years from Dayton, Ohio, to Pigeon Forge, Tennessee. It took five and a half to six hours, depending on traffic. If there was road construction or other problems, it might take six and a half hours. On this particular trip, he was driving his girlfriend on the route for a tour of the Smoky Mountains. He considered it a very routine road trip on well-known roads.

However, Jonathan and his friend encountered unusually severe thunderstorms along most of the route. Driving was difficult, and instead of speeding along at 60 to 70 miles per hour, he was driving between 25 to 40 most of the 337 miles. Sometimes, he was slowed to a mere 15 miles per hour. "I could barely see the road due to the extreme rain, thunder, lightning, and fog. It was very difficult to see so I had to drive agonizingly slow." He told his girlfriend, "We're never going to get there at this rate."

They finally drove out of the storms as they neared Pigeon Forge.

I looked at my watch and I was in shock. It was impossible. It only took a little over three hours to make the trip. There was no way. If you take 337 miles at 40 mph (and much of the time I was driving slower because of nearly zero visibility), it would have taken 8.42 hours. Even if I was averaging 55 MPH, it would take 6.1 hours. I was flabbergasted, but blew it off because I couldn't explain what happened.

It sounds as if Jonathan and his friend entered a space-time warp created by the storm.

Another Dimension

In this next story, two men driving at night in northern Michigan encounter a dense fog and not only realize that they leaped ahead in space, but seemingly find themselves temporarily in another dimension.

This story was sent to me from Gerald, who served in the military, where he worked as a scientist until his retirement. The incident took place in 1986.

"A friend and I were driving around with nothing specific in mind and realized that we had gone too far and all the local gas stations were closed," Gerald wrote.

They had two choices: either drive 22 miles north to Charlevoix or 17 miles south to Elk Rapids where there would be stations open later. After a short discussion, they decided to head south.

We turned south onto US 31 at M-88 in Eastport and at the 45th parallel we hit a very dense fog. We thought that was odd because the night sky had been very clear and calm at that point. My friend slowed down and within forty-five seconds we emerged from the fog to find that we were already on the outskirts of Elk Rapids. That freaked out both of us.

They continued a short distance to the gas station only to find it was closed, but all the lights were on. "We waited about five minutes when we both decided to head back north. Jokingly, I said we probably died and would see our wrecked car on our way home."

They got back to Central Lake, drove around town twice, and then parked by the lake to try to make sense of what they had experienced. "That's when we realized we hadn't seen another car or person or any living thing since the fog. My friend began to panic and I actually thought something was really off."

They waited at the lake for another hour until a car finally drove by, then they went home. "After that night, I tried to talk to my friend about what happened, but he refused to talk about it, and eventually stopped talking to me altogether. I've often thought about that night and after seeing your account, I can't help but see similarities."

Did Gerald and his friend temporarily move into another dimension, one that didn't quite fit their usual sense of reality? That's how it seemed to them.

"Time Is Space"

This story was sent to me in 2014 from Carmen of Pinole, California. She recalls an experience on a California freeway that happened in 1966. She makes no mention of weather conditions.

> I was leaving San Francisco and heading home. Traffic was heavy and I was barely moving and feeling frustrated. Suddenly, the traffic in front of me dissolved and I was look-ing at a large hourglass with sand dropping through the small opening. The words below the hourglass were "Time **is** space." Then the hourglass faded and I found myself miles down the road, nearing my exit for home. In a flash, I was at least thirty miles down the road. I was stunned!

Carmen was so excited that she told her friends and teachers who were amused. "The common response was: 'Uh, huh, and what were you smoking?' That in itself was funny, because I was always known as the girl who didn't drink or smoke anything. I'm now sixty-seven years old and still remember that experience like it was yesterday. It was so incredibly vivid."

Similar to others who wrote me, Carmen thanked me for recount-ing my story because I was the only other person who has ever described an experience that was somewhat similar to hers.

On the Ninth Hole

You don't have to be in a car to encounter the fog on land. In 2007, Hector Nunez and a friend were looking for a place to hang out one pleasant evening when they decided on the golf course adjacent to the Biltmore Hotel in Coral Gables, one of Miami's older neighbor-hoods. It was a place that Hector had visited from time to time since he was in high school. When the classic luxury hotel was new, Babe

Ruth used to play golf on the course. Keep in mind as you read this story that Hector and his friend Danny were, as Hector said, "stone-cold sober."

They were walking along the ninth hole of the course lost in conversation when suddenly they both stopped. "I clearly felt the eerie sensation of a large 'hand' slipping inside my head just behind my face and pressing against my brain. At the same time, the back of my head felt like it was burning," Hector recalled. He had never felt anything like that in his life. Before he could say anything, his friend said that he didn't want to go any farther because he saw "sparks" inside his eyes. "I realized that we had stopped walking and talking at the same moment. We felt two completely distinct sensations, but we both felt we shouldn't walk any farther."

That was when Hector noticed a dense wall of fog about 40 feet wide and 15 feet high. It was about 300 feet away between two trees. "After living in Florida my whole life, I can feel the air when it's conducive to fog. But this wasn't a fog night. I pointed it out to Danny, and he agreed it was odd. That's when the fog began to move toward us."

The wall of fog rolled up and down the small hills on the course. "It was snaking its way toward us. We hadn't even gotten over the shock if the initial 'high strangeness' that made us stop."

They began to walk backward as they watched it. The fog was about 100 feet from them when it stopped, then retreated back to the trees where they'd first seen it. "Danny and I tried to make sense of it, thinking of any scientific explanation to the movement of the fog, and to the feelings of danger. I was certainly no stranger to unexplained things happening, but nothing ever this intense."

Then the fog came out of the trees again, moving toward them, following the same path over the low hills. They began to walk backward again, this time faster, but keeping their gaze focused on the fog. "It came closer than before; its movements were deliberate. It was coming for us."

Hector noted that the fog could have gone in any direction or spread out and dissipated. "There was no dissipation. It was a single form of perfectly defined walls on all sides. We seemed to move too fast for it and it again began to creep slowly back the way it came."

They decided to listen to nature for hints as to what was going on. "Being a nature lover had taught me that the animals, insects, and birds would know of danger before you can sense it." They stopped talking and listened. "Nothing. No birds, no crickets, no wind. Just silence. We looked at each other, baffled, and decided it was time to leave. At that moment, out of the silence, a high-pitched screech tore through the night. It was coming from about 300 yards to the south, the direction we were facing."

Hector said the sound seemed to have an electronic tinge to it, as if it was a mix of biological and electronic sounds that merged together. Abruptly it stopped. But after a few seconds, another screech sounded to the east, this one closer. Then another and another until there was almost no breaks between screeches, and each one was nearer than the last.

"Three hundred yards to the south became 150 yards to the east, 75 yards, 50 yards, 20 yards to the northeast. Then the screech came at our feet, in the very grass in front of us. We were now facing north, as the sound encircled us. We moved the grass where the sound seemed to emanate from with our shoes. But there were no insects, no source to be found, nothing. We looked up and the wall of fog was coming at us faster than before and suddenly it was about four feet away. It had tricked us. It was intelligent."

Before they could move, the fog engulfed them, and Hector said it felt as if a wall of electricity had struck him.

Not like goose bumps or even chills from fear of the unexplained, or unknown. It hurt. Even fine hairs on my face and body were so charged they felt like hundreds of needles piercing my skin. The fog was dense and viscous, and moving in it felt surreal. It felt like thousands of eyes watching us and sizing us up as it swirled around us.

Danny screamed.

He was blinded by the same flashes of light inside of his eyes that stopped him earlier. He couldn't see anything and was terrified. I grabbed his arm and led him slowly through the fog toward the main buildings where I thought we would be safer. It was as though we were moving blindly through water. The sense of being watched was now unbearable. So I said aloud: "We are here with only peace and love in our hearts. We mean no harm. Let us be on our way."

They walked a ways further and reached the main paved path and the fog seemed to release them. They looked back and saw it retreating over the grassy mounds and back toward the nook in the trees where they had first seen it. They made their way quickly to Hector's car at the northern end of the golf course and sat there in disbelief for a few minutes. "We were taking in the magnitude of what had just happened to us. Then Danny pointed toward the golf course, and out of the darkness the fog was coming again. It made its way down the entire length of the lawn, through a tree line and chain-link fence. As I started the car, it was already in the parking lot. I sped away and have never encountered that fog again."

Hector sent his story to me in 2013 after reading *THE FOG*. A friend who knew about his experience had given it to him. Rob corresponded with Hector a number of times and Hector said they didn't experience any shift in time or instantaneous movement to another location. Both remain baffled by the experience, but neither he nor Danny had had any ill-effects in the aftermath. It happened, it was disturbing and shocking, then it was over.

Hector attributed intelligence and motivation to the fog, which I found intriguing, but puzzling. Were the two men only imagining that the fog was aware of them? If so, what caused the pain both experienced within their heads?

His description of the fog reminded me of the next story, except this this took place at sea...far from the Bermuda Triangle.

Time Slip on a Sailboat

In 2003, Rob and I flew from a private airport in Wellington, Florida, where I was living, to Fort Lauderdale. We landed at the site of the former Navy base, near the international airport, where Flight 19 originated in 1945. We were there to meet a Miami man who said he wanted to tell us about his strange experience with a fog while boating near Catalina Island off the coast of California.

Allen, a handsome man in his mid-40s at the time, was waiting for us when we arrived at a restaurant at the site of the old base. He had driven from Miami and was anxious to tell his story. We settled in a booth near a window that overlooked a runway on the former base. A short distance from the restaurant was the Flight 19 memorial—a large propeller attached to a stone monolith engraved with the names of the lost pilots.

After we ordered lunch, Allen prefaced his story by telling us he was a master electrical-mechanic engineer, a specialist in electromagnetism, and he worked at a biomedical company. On October 8, 1995, he joined a group of medical professionals for a day of sailing and fishing on a sailboat in the San Francisco Bay area. They left the dock at 8:15 a.m. under clear skies and light winds.

At 9:30 a.m., they anchored the craft and prepared their fishing gear. Within minutes, Allen and the others noticed the air shimmering above the water about 50 feet from the sailboat. It looked like a mirage created by solar radiation, as seen on roadways on hot days. But solar radiation doesn't occur above water, or such a short distance away, or in morning hours.

Everyone on board seemed mesmerized by the sight. As they peered at the shimmering mass, fog materialized, replacing the mirage. "It was low, thick, and rectangular-shaped, the top of it not more than three feet above the surface," Allen explained. "We all stared in fascination at the strange bed of fog as it moved toward the boat. The edge nearest the boat suddenly began to rise like a curtain. At the same time, it spread out until it was about a hundred feet wide and 70 feet high."

No one on board moved or talked. Everyone seemed entranced. The fog continued rising until it was as high as it was wide. The bed of fog disappeared and all that remained was the wall of fog. At first, the fog seemed nearly square, but after a few minutes the wall became oval-shaped and began to rotate clockwise. There was no wind, no sound, but the bright sunlight had vanished and the sky turned dusk-like. As the wall of fog rotated, the center spiraled inward, forming a revolving tunnel.

Suddenly, I realized that Allen was talking about something very familiar to me—the tunnel vortex. Even though there was no electrical storm underway, the tunnel and spiraling fog sounded very much like the entry point to the warp in the space-time continuum that I had experienced near Bimini.

I listened closely as Allen continued.

The fog kept coming closer and closer. It was threatening to swallow the sailboat. We quickly pulled up the anchor, started the engine, and fled. As soon as we left, the clear blue sky and sunshine returned. Everyone agreed that what we'd seen could've been a gate to another dimension or another time.

As our meals arrived, Allen added, "I wonder what would've happened if we'd gone into it? That's what I asked everyone on the boat, but no one responded."

By the time they returned to the marina where they had rented the sailboat, they were all nauseous and confused, as if they had just awakened from a trance. They were astonished that it was already 3 p.m. Somehow, four hours had disappeared. They sailed directly back to the marina after anchoring for about 20 minutes at the site of the fog. No one had caught any fish. No one had even thrown a line in the water. Where had the time gone? No one knew the answer.

Allen explained that he became more and more intrigued by what he had witnessed. He couldn't stop thinking about it. Again, that reminded me of the aftermath of my experience. There's something in nature that exists—passages to other dimensions, tears in the fabric and the space-time continuum. It exists beyond our current scientific knowledge and might account for many baffling disappearances.

Allen knew that he had seen and experienced something that couldn't be explained as any known weather phenomenon. He read everything he could find about mysteries of the sea, and he began studying quantum physics looking for an explanation. However, when he brought up the matter to others who had been on the boat, they didn't want to talk about it. They told him to forget about it. That, he knew, he would never do.

As we finished our lunch, I asked Allen about the four missing hours. Even though the fog didn't swallow the boat, the passengers were affected by it. What happened during that missing time? Maybe nothing. Maybe instead of losing track of four hours they leaped ahead in time. The gate or tunnel might have been a wormhole, a passage through time. Allen agreed that the time factor was key.

Before we parted ways, Allen vowed to go back and find the fog. This time he would pass through the gate. I told him that it's best to avoid electronic fog. The dangers are too great. He shook his head. "One way or another, I'm still going to find that fog. I don't care how long it takes."

I understand Allen's obsession, but not his willingness to dive into the fog. The last we heard, he hadn't found it. That's not surprising considering its elusiveness and inexplicable nature. The fog might find you, but you probably won't find the fog. At least, not very easily.

Lake Michigan Triangle

Lake Michigan is a vast inland body of water where numerous strange and mysterious events have been reported through the decades. They range from unusual disappearances to ghost ships and ghosts, to UFOs. So many people have observed UFOs over Lake Michigan that in the late 1990s, the Federal Aviation Administration created a special lake reporting service to catalog the sightings.

Encounters with fog resulting in space-time warps have also occurred. I became friends several years ago with Kathy Doore after we both appeared on a Bermuda Triangle documentary. "I've told this story many times over the years as my 'Lake Michigan Triangle' experience," she told me when we met for the first time.

"It was a perfect night for sailing with 7 to 10 knots of wind, flat seas, warm and sultry. It was mid-week and we had the lake to ourselves," Kathy wrote on her website *Labyrinthina.com* as she began relating her life-changing encounter with a mysterious fog that occurred in 1978.

She was aboard one of three classic wooden sailboats, part of a racing crew that competed every Sunday and practiced maneuvers during the week. They set sail near dusk for what should have been a routine cruise. However, about an hour out of port, they sailed into a dense fog. They couldn't see more than a few feet around them and feared they would crash into one another. The winds shifted about, filling one side of the mainsail, then the other.

She noticed the surface of the lake appeared eerily calm. Suddenly, she felt cold. "In fact, I was extremely cold. I was freezing."

She turned toward the helm to ask her crewmates if they were cold; to her astonishment they were no longer standing nearby. "One moment we had been crowded in the cockpit, and the next instant I was alone at the helm."

Dumfounded, she called out and found them standing up on the aft deck, where it was several degrees warmer. They seemed perplexed, and motioned for her to join them. That's when she realized that no one was steering the boat. "The Captain raised his arms high over his head, and said he hadn't been steering for ten minutes. Yet, I was certain that he had been standing next to me at the helm just a minute earlier."

Slowly, the boat carved a circle, then another and another without ever passing through the wind. Then, as abruptly as it had appeared, the fog vanished. That's when she saw the other two boats a few hundred yards away, rotating in the same way. Finally, the captains regained control of their vessels and sailed out of the slowly swirling vortex. All three boats turned and headed for port.

No one spoke as they sailed beneath the full moon. It was as if they were all under a spell. And that's when Kathy glimpsed her recently deceased father standing nearby. Her crewmates seemed lost in their own thoughts.

She noticed the lead boat enter the anchorage. It had once belonged to her team's captain and she knew it well. But as they entered the inlet, they found their old mooring empty, their sister-vessel nowhere in sight. They couldn't imagine where the others had gone. There *was* no place they could go. They cautiously navigated in and out of the moorings, searching for their companions.

Circling back a few minutes later, they were shocked to find that their sister-ship was not only tied up with sails stowed, but the crew was in their dingy rowing ashore, an impossibility in such a short span of time. Kathy and the others on her craft were baffled. It was as if time had been altered somehow.

After the third boat arrived, they all met onshore. The usually bois-terous group seemed dazed, Kathy recalled. They wanted nothing more than to go home and go to sleep. To Kathy's surprise, it was after mid-night. They had left port nearly six hours earlier, but she was certain they had been out no more than three or four hours. As the weeks passed, Kathy realized they couldn't account for a good portion of the evening.

The following Sunday as they prepared for a big race, Kathy brought up the unusual events from their previous sail. But to her utter astonishment no one would talk about it. They acted as if nothing out of the ordinary had occurred.

It seemed the others had blocked out the memory. Through the years, she came to believe that the events of that night might have been for my benefit. After all, she was the only one who was willing to talk about what happened, possibly the only one who remembered.

Kathy died in the spring of 2015. She was an intrepid explorer of the weird and strange, and took numerous trips to Peru, where she explored the ancient spiritual site of Marcahuasi. Her coffee table book by the same name introduced the Western world to the site at which large boulders appear to resemble animals and mystical creatures.

On the evening of April 8th, my wife, Lynn, and I, along with a dozen others, held a memorial for Kathy on a catamaran. Kathy had requested that her ashes be scattered at sea. Considering her love of sailing, the edge of the Bermuda Triangle seemed a fitting place for the memorial. The weather was beautiful, and before we departed, Rob's wife, Trish, said that Kathy might put in an appearance. I had no idea how that would happen, but as we headed out to sea, Rob pointed out a pair of contrails in the sky that formed a "V," as if pointing our way. In the middle of the two contrails was a small fleecy cloud vaguely shaped like an angel. Lynn took a photo of it and when we uploaded it to a computer for a better look, we noticed a distinct white orb on the lower left side of the cloud. It seemed as though Kathy indeed had made an appearance.

<hr />

I like to think that electronic fog is a meteorological phenomenon. But there's another aspect to electronic fog and mysterious events related to it that comes up again and again: the UFO factor. Although I've touched on this topic and its relationship to space-time warps, I'll take a much closer and more personal look at the UFO phenomenon in the next chapter.

Chapter
8

Close Encounters of the Bermuda Triangle Kind

I have a confession to make: I never wanted to write about UFOs. I knew that they were part of the legend of the Bermuda Triangle and had come into popular awareness through the writing of Charles Berlitz and his avid researcher Manson Valentine, as well as other writers. In the legend, the Bermuda Triangle serves as an underwater base for UFOs and as a portal or entry point from which they arrive from other planets or other dimensions, possibly the future, or even the past. As I previously mentioned, Dr. Valentine saw the Bermuda Triangle as the locale where UFOs moved between the lost continent of Atlantis and other realms.

I don't know if any of that is true. What I do know is that in the aftermath of my mysterious flight through the heart of the Bermuda Triangle phenomenon I have encountered UFOs in a very personal way. In fact, I wouldn't be telling the entire breadth of my story if I ignored the controversial question of whether or not we are being visited by beings from somewhere other than Earth.

Night Flight

In January 1971, just a month after I flew through the dangerous storm cloud and seemingly punctured the space-time continuum, I experienced a second close encounter with death. This time it arrived in the form of an enormous, mysterious craft.

It was a perfectly clear night, great for a flight. My girlfriend had never flown in a small plane at night and decided she wanted to join me. It was about 9 p.m. when we lifted off from West Palm Beach and flew south along Florida's Gold Coast. I kept climbing to get a better view of the city lights. We went all the way to 10,000 feet before leveling off. After flying directly over Miami International Airport, we headed east over the Atlantic and left the maze of city lights behind to enjoy a flight under the canopy of stars.

We were nearing the same area where I had exited the tunnel vortex when I noticed a bright orange star to the southeast that I thought might be a planet. It was just above the horizon and, as I focused on it, I realized it was moving. Just as I pointed it out, the orange beacon suddenly grew larger and we watched in amazement as it moved directly toward us at an incredible speed.

Within 10 seconds, it was right in front of us and it was enormous, more than 300 feet wide and 90 feet thick. It was bright amber, metallic—about three times the size of a Boeing 747—and filled the entire windshield. I thought we were about to be demolished. Just before impact, I veered sharply to the left, turning as hard as possible, but I thought we had no chance of avoiding a collision.

Somehow the craft avoided knocking us out of the sky. I looked back after making the turn and expected to see the UFO moving in a westward direction. To my surprise, it was gone. I had no idea what happened to it. In retrospect, it could have lifted straight up and soared skyward. We were just relieved to be alive.

Years later, I received an email from a man named Ted. He had seen a Bermuda Triangle documentary in which I described that UFO encounter. He wrote: "When the UFO was in front of you, then disappeared behind you, that was the point at which you were taken. Tests were run and then you were released. They try very hard to put people back where they found them."

He went on to say that he knew what he was talking about because he had been abducted numerous times. "The technology exists for them to take you, the plane, and all inside the vehicle. The vehicle you saw is actually only the part of it that exists inside our dimension. It's incredibly huge. Your plane would be like a matchbox inside your car."

I've seen lots of UFOs, but I don't remember seeing any aliens. However, oddly enough, I do seem to have a knack for knowing when UFOs will appear, as you'll see in the next story.

Predicting UFOs

In the aftermath of my Bermuda Triangle encounter, I had a number of experiences in which I sensed events before they happened. The first time, which I wrote about in Chapter 3, was my vision of meeting Dr. Valentine and eating dinner at a restaurant with him.

Three years later, it happened again. This time it related to a UFO. My wife, Lynn, and I took a trip to North Carolina on a commercial airliner; before we left home I sensed we were going to see a UFO. I felt certain about it and knew it would happen on the return flight. I was feeling excited about it and made sure we got seats on the left side of the plane. That way we could look out toward the Bermuda Triangle as we flew south along the coast toward West Palm Beach.

My camera was resting on my lap when we noticed a disc-shaped object less than a mile away. Lynn was at the window seat and I handed her the camera. Other passengers also saw it.

It looked like the craft I had seen on that night flight. It was the same amber color and seemed to glow from within, creating a metallic appearance. It also had a similar bulge at the top—like a cockpit—as the unidentified craft that had nearly collided with me. Lynn took several pictures of it. The craft appears tiny in the photos, just as an airplane would from a mile away. But the distinct shape of the craft is clearly visible with the aid of a magnifying glass.

The sighting was just the beginning. The next day I had a strong urge to go to the beach that evening and watch the night sky. I just knew at least one UFO would appear. The weather was clear, visibility more than 10 miles. We headed to Delray Beach with binoculars. Not long after arriving, my hunch proved correct. We spotted a reddish glowing object moving rapidly north to south off the coast. We watched it for about 10 seconds. Just as it disappeared to the south another one appeared from the north, following the same path. Then another and another.

They were about 10 miles offshore, and through the zoom-lens binoculars, appeared disc-shaped. They looked similar to the ones I had seen the night before. Finally, a fifth object appeared and made a remarkable maneuver. Just as it was about to pass by, traveling at about 500 miles an hour, it carved an incredible 90-degree turn and flew toward shore. When it neared the beach, it flashed a blue light several times, then shot by directly overhead and was quickly out of sight. It was an astonishing experience that I'll never forget.

Seeing a UFO, for most people, is a rare, unusual experience. But not so much for me. I've seen UFOs at least 20 times. The unusual part of the encounters for me is when I'm somehow able to predict their appearance, as I did on the commercial flight and at the beach the next night. There was another instance when I predicted to a skeptic that we would see a UFO from his party boat. It happened a few months after the two sightings I just described.

I was talking to my friend Tim about the mystery of the Bermuda Triangle and my experiences, and I could tell that he doubted what I was saying. Tim was an accomplished sea captain and had been sailing in the Bermuda Triangle for years without experiencing anything out of the ordinary.

While Tim was talking about plans for a cruising party on his sailboat during the upcoming weekend, I suddenly felt excited and knew that we would see something unusual during the trip. I interrupted him and said, "This Saturday night, when we go out on your boat, you and everyone else will see an unusual light in the direction of Bimini."

Tim laughed and neither one of us mentioned it again until the night of the cruise. About a dozen people gathered on the sailboat that Saturday afternoon and headed down the Intracoastal to the inlet at Boca Raton, then out into the ocean. We sailed a few miles offshore to the edge of the Gulf Stream and headed north toward Palm Beach on a beautiful tropical night.

I had almost forgotten about the prediction when someone yelled out that they saw a strange light over the ocean. It was in the direction of Bimini, but it wasn't like any of the UFOs I'd seen. It looked more like a beam of white light being projected for several miles from about 3,000 feet above the sea.

The beam appeared to be about 10 miles away and was slowly rotating like a luminous second hand on an enormous sky clock. As we watched, it made three complete revolutions, each one taking about two minutes before the light disappeared. There were scattered cumulus clouds in the area and when the beam hit the clouds it illuminated them and cut off the rest of the beam. I asked Tim if it could be the Great Isaac lighthouse near Bimini, but he said it would be impossible to see it because it was 50 miles away.

I suggested that it was some sort of atmospheric reflection of the lighthouse beam that we were seeing, but Tim rejected that idea. He had seen the lighthouse beam many times at night so he knew what it looked like. He said it was the strangest light he had ever seen in all his years of sailing and that he had no idea what it could be.

After that experience Tim changed his mind about the Bermuda Triangle. Whenever the subject came up and he was around, I used to enjoy teasing him by saying, "Tim saw the light!" He would always agree and say, "Gernon showed me the light."

The Attraction

What is it that attracts UFOs and USOs to the Bermuda Triangle? The key factor, it seems, is that the area possesses a special magnetism that can trigger sudden severe magnetic storms and cause malfunctions in electronic equipment. Valentine believed that these magnetic anomalies were the result of both natural forces and a product of the UFOs themselves. Berlitz quotes him in *Without a Trace*: "'Space engineers may be utilizing the electrical potential of a very special area of the Earth.... These inter-dimensional craft may be quite invisible to us while their presence in our atmosphere is being felt magnetically."

In fact, Valentine believed that the original elliptical cloud that I passed in my encounter—the one I thought was a lenticular cloud—actually harbored a UFO that was either arriving or departing.

When Berlitz asked Valentine what he thought caused strange disappearances in the Bermuda Triangle, Valentine responded in a comment published near the end of Berlitz's book, *Without a Trace*. He said:

> Either the magnetic fields are the result of sporadic, perhaps seasonal buildup of geophysical origin, or they are the concomitant effects of UFO activity. Possibly a combination of both agencies can occur. Another important aspect to consider is the likelihood of magnetic, cyclonic storms initiated by either condition. Like the tornado, the magnetic vortex would be self-augmenting and could well bring about an inter-dimensional transition for anyone caught up in it. The experience of Bruce Gernon is a case in point.

Gian J. Quasar, author of *Into the Bermuda Triangle: Pursuing the Truth Behind the World's Greatest Mystery,* is convinced that UFOs play an important role in the mystery.

> ...[T]he mere presence of flying saucers, their shape, speed, and the fact that they seem to be here, led us to considering electromagnetism and gravity as means of propulsion. Every bit of our research has led us to believe that such propulsion is possible, that discs are the best shape for this propulsion, and that phenomenal speeds and perhaps some very novel conduits of travel are easily attained....

Quasar, who is familiar with my experience, went on to say: "It is possible that Bruce Gernon actually flew along a field line briefly while in a magnetic vortex caused by charged particles swirling around the line of force, proving perhaps that one day we can project matter along lines of magnetic force."

In addition, Quasar relates the story in his book of two fishermen from Indiana, who were cruising to the Bahamas from West Palm Beach, when they encountered something luminous in the sky. On June 25, 2001, Paul Vance and Doug Gerdon were 11 miles off shore in Vance's 26-foot sailboat, *Rare Form,* when they noticed a single light 3- to 5,000 feet in altitude. Vance, a commercial pilot, was well qualified to estimate size, distance, and speed.

At first, they assumed they were looking at an airplane, but when the light turned downward, they thought it might be a helicopter with a searchlight. As they observed the light under cloudless conditions, a swirling mist engulfed the light as it slowly drifted down. Initially, the light hovered above the area where the mist had formed, then lowered into it. "The whole mass of mist glowed for a short time, then dissipated along with the light," Vance said. He added that it looked like the light was passing through a misty tunnel before it disappeared.

The entire incident took between two and three minutes, and the boat's engine lost power about the time they saw the light. The engine continued to run rough, so they sailed back to West Palm Beach. "When the engine faltered and I saw that swirling mist, I thought to myself, 'My God, there's something to this Bermuda Triangle stuff!'"

In *The Bermuda Triangle,* Charles Berlitz wrote that "no investigator of events in the Bermuda Triangle can avoid confronting reports of UFOs." He noted that they were seen not only in the sky, but below the water, suggesting the idea of an underwater base in the Bermuda Triangle.

Unidentified Submerged Objects (USOs)

Just as UFOs and the Bermuda Triangle saga seem inseparable, the same can be said for USOs. Even though I've never seen a UFO dive into the ocean or rise out of it, USOs could be a key factor in the mystery. It's worthwhile to explore the topic here because of how it relates to Andros Island, where my Bermuda Triangle encounter originated (and it is the subject of the next chapter).

For example, this report was filed on *www.waterufo.net* by a passenger on a cruise ship, the *Costa Fortuna,* who woke up at 5:30 a.m. on December 18, 2007. The woman took out her binoculars to look at the stars through the large window in her room. In the distance, she saw what initially looked like another ship in distress.

All the lights on the ship suddenly started blinking off and on. One row of lights was orange-yellow, and below it another row was a neon blue-green. She said the ship wasn't moving, and as the cruise ship approached, something strange happened: "The ship suddenly started to change shape and color. It became a round object and began to lift off the water."

She went on to say that six balloon-shaped, metallic objects emerged from "smoke" surrounding the craft, and lifted skyward.

She initially hesitated in sharing her experience because she thought people would think she was dreaming or hallucinating. She described herself as a professional person with a PhD and a respected person in her community. Eventually, her story found its way to Carl Feindt at *waterufo.net*. Feindt's site is probably the best source of stories about USOs and contains a massive database.

My guess is that fog or steam, rather than smoke, surrounded the craft as it changed form. Dr. Valentine collected dozens of reports of UFOs and USOs, and found that localized fog and electromagnetic anomalies seemed to be present during so-called "arrivals and departures."

Among cases Valentine examined—and Berlitz included in *The Bermuda Triangle*—were reports by fishermen who had spotted huge crafts moving underwater. Michael Kunhe of Miami was a few miles off Fowey Rock, Key Biscayne, in May 1975 when he noticed a massive gray-white object beneath his boat that looked like an underwater cloud. The object "fritzed" his depth-finder and sonar, and he decided to get out of the area quickly.

Berlitz also wrote about another fisherman, Don Delmonico, who in 1973 saw something very similar near Bimini. The object was light gray, about 100 to 200 feet long, and seemed to be smooth, without fins, portholes, elevators, superstructure, or any type of propulsion. It raced beneath his 35-foot boat, moving about 75 miles per hour.

One of the best documented USO cases, cited by Berlitz in *Inside the Bermuda Triangle*, involved the U.S. Navy, and occurred in February 1963. That month, a fleet of Navy vessels—ships, submarines, and aircraft—were positioned off the coast of Puerto Rico performing training in anti-submarine maneuvers with the USS WASP (cv-18), an aircraft carrier, serving as the command ship.

During the exercise, the vessels detected an unknown sonar target moving in the area. One of the submarines moved to pursue and investigate, but the submarine couldn't catch it. The fleet tracked the unknown object and recorded that it moved at more than 150 knots—more than 170 miles per hour—and descended to the bottom of the Puerto Rico Trench, the deepest valley in the North Atlantic with depths of more than 28,000 feet. At the time of the incident, the top speed of submarines was 45 knots and their greatest depth was 3,000 feet. It almost seemed as if the USO was playing with the fleet. *Try tracking this maneuver for your training exercise!*

I suspect that such encounters played an important role in the Navy's decision to create a permanent base in 1969 in the Bahamas on Andros Island, located at the edge of another ocean trench, known as the Tongue of the Ocean. In the next chapter, we will go there and find out more about the Navy base and mysterious happenings in the area.

Chapter
9

Return to Andros

June in south Florida is the beginning of the rainy season, when typically there will be a downpour in the afternoon and a half hour later the sun will come out. On one particular day in mid-June of 2003, scattered showers arrived early and by 10 a.m. were clearing up as I drove 30 miles to North Perry Airport. I would meet the pilot of a twin-engine Piper Aztec, who would fly me and a crew from the Discovery Channel to Andros Island. It would be the first time in more than 30 years that I would return to the site of my mysterious experience in the Bermuda Triangle.

En route, I noticed a rainbow. I moved beyond it, then noticed another one, and another after that. Altogether, I saw five rainbows on that drive. The astonishing thing was that the last rainbow arced right onto the tarmac at North Perry Airport from where we would depart for Andros. I took that as a good sign.

The flight was uneventful until we were approaching Andros and close to where I saw the saucer-shaped cloud that would form the mother storm on my flight in 1970. That's when something caught my eye as I gazed down at the pale blue waters to the Great Bahama Bank, the shallow limestone platform on which Andros rests.

En route to the airport to return to Andros Island after many years, Gernon sees five rainbows, the last one ending on the airport tarmac.
Photo credit: Bruce Gernon.

"Look down there. Look at the water. Do you see that?" I pointed at two large white patches that looked like clouds against the tranquil aqua sea. "That's the white water I told you about."

Years ago, I photographed mysterious areas of white water in the expanse between Florida and the Bahamas. I've often wondered if that water has something to do with the Bermuda Triangle phenomenon. The plane swept low, making several passes over the patches of white water as I snapped more photos with my 35mm camera. Breaking waves, of course, make white water, but this water was flat and placid. When the pictures were developed, they looked like great white whales on the surface of the sea.

We continued on to Andros, the largest and least populated island in the Bahamas, and undoubtedly the most mysterious. Within minutes we reached the western shore and flew over the dense interior forest, which is uninhabited and largely inaccessible. It consists of more than 700 islets covered by pines and mangroves, all surrounded by estuaries and expansive tidal swamplands. The island's numerous blue holes lead into an intricate underwater cave system that honeycomb the island.

When Christopher Columbus landed in the Bahamas, the islands were populated by a people who called themselves the *Lukku-cairi*, or "Island People," and their name for Andros was *Lucayoneque*, or "Island of Islands." The Spanish renamed it *Isla de Spiritu Sanctu* (Island of the Holy Spirit). In 1670, the island was granted to six British lords and renamed as Andros Island after Sir Edmund Andros.

Large patches of white water appear on calm seas in the Bermuda Triangle.

Mythology of Andros

Andros is the home of two mythical creatures. The Chickcharney is an elfin being, either furry or feathered, three feet tall with an owl-like appearance, but monkey-like behavior. It has one red eye and three-toed claws, and a prehensile tail that allows it to hang from trees.

Chickcharneys are said to build nests by joining two pine trees together at the top. According to legend, those who treat a Chickcharney well will be awarded with good luck. Treat one badly and you can expect hard times. According to locals, Chickcharneys are still occasionally spotted in the forest. They suggest carrying flowers or bits of bright cloth when touring the island in order to charm these mischievous creatures.

There's also the enormous Lusca, which is half-octopus, half-shark, a monster of the deep that supposedly resides in the blue holes. The Lusca is said to span 200 feet with tentacles extending 75 feet from its body. It's also been described as a multi-headed monster, a dragon-like creature, or an evil spirit. Take your pick.

However, I was more interested in another part of the mystique of Andros Island, a more concrete one.

After passing over the 35 miles of forest, we flew over Andros Town on the east coast, the island's main population center, in which about 2,500 of the 7,300 residents live. To me, the town seemed frozen in time. It didn't look any different than when I was there decades prior. From the air it didn't appear any larger or smaller. There is no downtown, no commercial buildings. Just a few small shops and three or four restaurants.

Of more interest was another community, a secret U.S. Navy base, located about a mile from the town. The base itself is not secret. It's difficult to hide a complex of buildings from the spying eye of Google Earth and the windows of passing airplanes. However, what they *do* at the base—or some of what they do—is the secret part. To that end, the Atlantic Undersea Test and Evaluation Center, or AUTEC, has been called the "Underwater Area 51," referring to the Nevada Air Force base that is often linked to UFOs.

AUTEC borders the Tongue of the Ocean, a deep trench that runs 150 miles long and 20 miles wide. Its depth varies from 3,600 feet in the south to 6,600 feet in the north. Although the land area of the base is only about one square mile, AUTEC extends out from the island into the Tongue of the Ocean. It includes a secret underwater submarine dock that is nearly the size of the base's land area.

We circled low over the base after obtaining clearance from both the Nassau Tower and the Miami Air Traffic Control. I was surprised that we were able to enter the air space over the base. But our pilot, Stuart Hanley, had 25 years of flying in the Bahamas and the Caribbean and had no trouble getting the go-ahead.

Visitors are not allowed at AUTEC unless sponsored by a base employee. In the early 1970s, I had access to the base through a friend who worked there as a mathematician. So I was familiar to some extent with the physical setting, but not much at all about what goes on there. I noticed that they had added a huge helicopter pad large enough for a dozen military choppers to land at the same time. A Blackhawk was winding down on one pad as we passed over.

AUTEC publicly states that it involves testing underwater warfare weapons, primarily torpedoes and mines. It also works with submarines, unmanned underwater vehicles, electronic warfare, and underwater acoustics. With a secret base located in the heart of the Bermuda Triangle, it's not surprising that AUTEC has been compared to Area 51 and supposedly conducts mysterious "black bag" projects (secret research with untraceable funding).

According to the legend, the secret side of AUTEC has something to do with strange fogs, malfunction electronic equipment, and even teleportation and time travel. Those projects supposedly are related to research that started with the work of radio pioneer Nikola Tesla. According to legend, AUTEC carries on the legacy of the infamous

Philadelphia Experiment—a secret Navy invisibility experiment that supposedly occurred during the 1940s and resulted in teleportation of a ship to another site, among other astonishing effects.

Considering that UFOs and USOs have been spotted near the base and that much of the base area is located underwater, it's easy to see why AUTEC has been called the Underwater Area 51. Of course, sightings of UFOs and USOs near the base don't necessarily mean that the Navy is involved with aliens and their crafts. It could be that visitors from elsewhere are monitoring the base's activities. In fact, some of the most baffling UFO cases have occurred near military bases, especially ones involved with nuclear weapons.

In the early morning hours of March 16, 1967, maintenance and security forces at Malmstrom Air Force reported sightings of UFOs hovering above the Minuteman missile sites. By 8:30 a.m., one of the missiles had become inoperable. In quick succession, the entire flight of 10 ICBM missiles went down. Power had not been lost to the site. Instead, each of their guidance and control systems malfunctioned and they were inoperable.

Twenty miles away at another missile site, security personnel also reported UFOs over the base, including one that hovered at the front gate. At the same time, the base's Minuteman missiles shutdown. In spite of the presence of UFOs, witnessed by numerous airmen and security personnel, the Air Force has never provided an explanation as to why the missiles simultaneously shut down at the two sites.

Tales From Andros

Civilian workers at AUTEC are the least likely personnel to know about the base's secret projects, unless they are directly involved. But civilian employees, especially former employees, have been the ones most willing to talk about UFOs and USOs. In fact, in one instance, a civilian worker visiting the West Palm Beach area recognized me from my appearances on documentaries and within minutes related an extraordinary story.

I was eating dinner at a sports bar when I noticed a man on the opposite side of the horseshoe staring at me. The man whispered something to the bartender, who then came over and asked me if I was the pilot who had the strange Bermuda Triangle experience. I said I was, and the bartender told me a gentleman across the bar said he worked at AUTEC on Andros Island and would like to talk to me.

Because there was an open seat next to the man during the crowded dinner hour, I joined the stranger. The man, who was wearing a t-shirt with an AUTEC logo emblazoned on it, told me that he was still employed at the secret Navy base and wasn't going to tell me his name. (We'll call him Earl.) He said he has had two unusual experiences while working as a civilian employee, but he was only willing to tell me one of them.

Earl explained he was working as an engineer on a submarine near the south end of the Tongue of the Ocean when the electronic equipment suddenly acted as if it were possessed. It was as if they had entered a space where the known laws of physics collapsed. Several seconds passed, then everything returned to normal—everything except that they were now near the north end of the Tongue of the Ocean, about 100 miles from where they had been moments earlier. The shift in positions was documented on radar. No one could explain what had happened.

I was fascinated and could only imagine what the second story—the one Earl wouldn't talk about—must involve. Was this incident part of an AUTEC secret experiment—one similar to the Philadelphia Experiment—and one that Earl and others aboard the sub didn't know about? Or was something else involved, something alien and powerful that existed deep within Tongue of the Ocean?

Even though the incident took place deep below the surface, I couldn't help thinking about the similarity to my own encounter that began on Andros Island. Like Earl, I experienced a sudden shift in location after my electronic equipment malfunctioned. In my case, it was near Bimini to 10 miles from Miami Beach, a distance of 90 miles.

From the Depths

Several years after my trip with the Discovery Channel, Rob and I flew to Andros Island for the History Channel's *UFO Hunters* series. As a result of that experience, which I'll talk about later in the chapter, we met two former AUTEC civilian employees who told us about their astonishing experiences.

Curt Rowlett was working on a ship as a civil engineer for AUTEC in 1985 when a USO was picked up on radar. "One evening, we pulled out of the dock, and suddenly out of nowhere, a radar contact popped up directly in front of our ship. It appeared to be a land mass where no land mass should exist." Within seconds, the massive object faded and disappeared from radar, suggesting that whatever it was had sunk into the depths.

That sighting could have been a radar glitch. However, it wasn't the first time that Rowlett had witnessed an inexplicable "land mass" in the depths off Andros Island. He had experienced one five years earlier, while in the Coast Guard. "We pulled away from the AUTEC dock well after nightfall, and I was at the helm watch," he recalled. "Suddenly, the officer of the watch told me, 'Hey, I've got a radar contact showing land dead ahead about three miles.' That was patently impossible, because we were in the Tongue of the Ocean and it's a thousand fathoms deep."

The object was "the size of an island," Rowlett said, a blob on the radar measuring between one and two miles in diameter. Meanwhile, the compass needle lashed about wildly. Rowlett didn't know what was happening and wondered if he was in danger.

About three minutes later, when they were about a mile and a half from the "land mass," it vanished from radar and the compass stopped spinning. He noted that radar only picks up objects at sea level, so whatever it was might have descended out of range. The captain was awakened, and he took the incident seriously, entering it in the ship's log. The radar was tested the next day and found to be in perfect operating condition.

The Torpedo That Wasn't

Another former AUTEC employee had a similar experience, but this one was much closer. Dave Malcolm, a weapons technician at the secret base, was working on a torpedo retriever boat in early 1973. It was a typical mission and the vessel had stopped in the testing range about 20 miles from Andros to collect a torpedo. Malcolm stepped out on a platform that extended from the boat just below the surface of the water for easy retrieval of spent weapons. Suddenly, he saw a massive structure rising rapidly directly behind the boat.

Visibility in the water was good, but the day was somewhat gray and the water a bit rough. "I clearly saw what at first appeared to me to be a pipeline and remember thinking: *What's a pipeline doing in the middle of the water?*" As the object continued rising, he realized it wasn't a pipeline and that it was about to collide with their boat.

Then, abruptly, it stopped just below the surface. Malcolm couldn't tell how wide it was or how far below the surface it extended. It was much thicker than a torpedo and much narrower than a submarine, two objects that were familiar to him in his work. It seemed to hover for a few moments, then slowly retreated, sinking out of sight.

He had no time to call out to anyone, and no one else saw the object. Thinking about his orders, he decided not to say anything about it. "This was during a time when a top secret clearance was taken very seriously and it was hammered into us that we would never discuss what we did or saw. I still have the security manual that describes the term in federal prison for violating the need to know."

Malcolm had never seen anything like it and had no idea what it was. He thought at the time that it might be a secret experimental craft, but over the years his doubts have grown. Secret crafts, he noted, usually become public knowledge after a time, but in all these years he hasn't seen or heard of any underwater craft similar to what he witnessed that day.

Considering its cylindrical shape, it's possible to imagine that Malcolm was looking at the outer edge of a saucer-shaped craft that had risen vertically. In other words, most of the vessel was below the surface, out of sight, and he saw only the rim. It's crew or sensors detected the boat and it retreated into the depths.

Electronic Warfare Threat Simulator

AUTEC activities take place not only underwater in the Tongue of the Ocean, but also in the air. To that end, electromagnetic signals are sent out into the atmosphere through high-powered amplifiers that are components of the base's Electronic Warfare Simulator. According to a public document, the simulator "generates complex, dynamic, electromagnetic signal environments at the radio frequency (RF) level." The system is housed in a dome on a 74-foot tower. Interestingly, one of the former civilian AUTEC employees mentioned to Rob that when he worked on the base, the most secretive area—where only those with the highest level of clearance could enter—was the dome.

The simulator is capable of illuminating aircrafts, surface vessels, and submarines as they move through the "tracking range," the surrounding area where the base's activities take place. There is no mention of any danger posed by these energy fields to the vessels or aircrafts being tracked or to other passing airplanes and ships. However, when we left Andros after our *UFO Hunters* escapade, we flew very close to the AUTEC base and encountered something unexpected, as we'll explain at the end of the chapter.

The Bermuda Triangle might be a large-scale laboratory where electromagnetic energy released naturally from the earth or radiating from the sun as a result of solar flares produce electronic fog and other mysterious phenomena. But nature might be getting a helping hand from humankind. Radio waves and electromagnetic energy generated at the AUTEC facility might instigate the unusual atmospheric conditions or enhance the conditions already created by nature.

Passing Out

I doubt that the military is intentionally endangering people traveling through the Bermuda Triangle. However, it is certainly possible that the atmospheric experiments that produce EM fields could inadvertently create mysterious effects. I recall an odd experience that took place near Andros Island about a year after my flight through the electronic fog. I was flying home from a trip to Providenciales with my longtime friend, Dennis Morley, and our two girlfriends when the incident occurred.

We were cruising at 10,500 feet, enjoying ourselves as we watched the islands of the Bahamas pass by on a beautiful afternoon. As we approached Andros from the southeast, we were flying over the deep water of the Tongue of the Ocean. I had just mentioned that we were getting close to the area where I'd first encountered a strange cloud the year before.

When I looked over my shoulder at the two young women in the backseat, they had both passed out. Dennis and I laughed about it. Then, just a minute later, Dennis suddenly fell asleep right in the midst of our conversation.

I thought it strange that they all passed out just as we were approaching Andros. I couldn't understand why they were so tired.

We had all gone to bed early the night before and slept late that day. I tried talking to Morley, but he was in a deep sleep and didn't wake up. It bothered me because he was supposed to be my copilot.

They all woke up about an hour later. We had traveled about 200 miles and were over the Gulf Stream and descending into Palm Beach. I had no idea why I remained awake while the others passed out.

Did the location of the plane near AUTEC have anything to do with my initial experience or the odd behavior of my passengers a year later? It would be presumptuous and speculative to say so. Yet, there is something eerie about the fact that the last person I spoke to before taking off from Andros and entering the "mother storm" was a friend, John Woolbright, who worked at AUTEC.

I've never wanted to believe that the government has anything to do with what happened to me. I tend to believe Gian Quasar, author of *Into the Bermuda Triangle,* who wrote on his website, "It's highly probable that nature can form these fields on her own and create the right situation for a ship or aircraft to either totally disintegrate or disappear and show up in another dimension."

That said, I also recall a scientist associated with Palm Beach State College telling me in 1973 that I had most likely flown into an AUTEC experiment. I rejected the idea. I didn't want to believe it then and I still don't want to believe it now. But through the years, it keeps coming back to AUTEC.

UFO Hunters

In April 2009, I returned again to Andros. This time Rob and I flew from West Palm Beach to Andros in my Cessna 182 to be interviewed for an episode of the History Channel's *UFO Hunters.* Our wives, Trish and Lynn, joined us. As we might have expected, the trip was not without its share of strange events.

On my previous trip with the Discovery Channel we simply passed over the island and returned to South Florida. This time we were landing and staying a couple of nights. As we approached the island, the water suddenly glowed with a neon brilliance. It was like seeing special effects in a movie—the Northern Lights shimmering on the surface of the water. The phenomenon lasted several seconds; we all saw it, but didn't know what to make of it. We figured it was just a reflection of sunlight, yet I felt that somehow it was significant.

Luminous neon lights symbolize illumination of the darkness, exposing what is hidden. It was a perfect metaphor for a television show that was setting out to shed light on a secret military base that might have something to do with UFOs. The episode was not only about the Bermuda Triangle, but also about AUTEC and how the base had come to be rumored as the underwater Area 51.

Our interviews on the beach with the *UFO Hunter* cast—Bill, Pat, and Ted—went well. They were especially interested in my story because my flight had originated on Andros. They also interviewed former civilian AUTEC employees they had flown to the island and others with stories or information. However, Bill Birnes, the lead cast member, wanted to get inside the base, take a tour, and possibly interview the commander. He knew it would be a challenge. No cable channel documentary film crews had ever gotten approval to film inside, and repeated requests by the producers to be the first to do so were ignored. The powers-that-be at AUTEC didn't say no; they didn't respond at all. Maybe it was the name of the show, or just the base policy not to conduct interviews.

In spite of the rejection, Birnes still wanted to try to get inside at least for a tour. We were with him at the time, and he invited us to come along. So we crowded into a rented jeep and headed for the gate. We parked on the side of the road a couple of hundred yards away and began our approach on foot with the camera crew.

We hadn't gotten very far when a chopper lifted off from the base and hovered over the gate. Was it an attempt to intimidate us and possibly block out any audio if the crew filmed near the gate? We kept moving forward until two cop cars arrived. Instead of pulling directly into the gate, they both parked across the gate, as if forming a barrier.

At that point, Birnes decided it was time to back off. Whether or not the activity was directed at our approach, it was a clear sign we weren't welcome. We probably wouldn't have seen much had we gotten inside. Tours of the base are extremely limited. As one long-time civilian employee at the base put it: "You don't get very far. You don't see much and you don't learn anything more than what is already public knowledge." Still, it would've been worth the trip to see Birnes ask the commander of the base about UFOs and aliens. But it didn't happen.

However, there is a postscript to the failed visit to the base. Four months after our attempt, Rob and Trish walked into a crowded out-door bar in Sarasota, Florida. They had spent the day helping their daughter move into her dorm for her second year of college and were ready to kick back and listen to some music.

They looked for an empty table and settled on what was available, a pair of stools on a partially occupied high-top table. They ordered beers as a band played raucous cover tunes from the '60s and '70s. They didn't know anyone in the bar and had no plans to meet anyone.

Considering those circumstances, what happened in the next hour seemed highly unlikely. They were about to penetrate the wall of official silence surrounding the secret base on Andros. The man seated across from them with a raspberry martini in hand had just retired from the Navy and his last assignment was as the commander of AUTEC.

To their amazement, and possibly because he was retired and enjoying the evening out, Commander "Richard" was willing to talk about the base—at least to a limited degree. He was also very curious about their visit to Andros with *UFO Hunters.* If he thought it was hilarious that the program was about UFOs, he didn't reveal it by his expression or comments. He looked as if he was about to say something important in response when the band kicked into "Honky Tonk Woman" and he leaned back into his chair and looked over at the band.

But Rob got his attention again and raised his voice over the music. He told the commander that some former AUTEC civilian employees had talked about sightings of UFOs and USOs near the base. Commander Richard studied him a moment, then said: "You know what, Rob, I think I need another martini."

Finally, when the band took a break, Rob pursued the matter again. He asked if Commander Richard knew that some people called AUTEC the Navy's equivalent to Area 51. The former commander didn't smile or frown. His expression gave away nothing at all. But he seemed less than forthcoming as he responded. He shook his head and said: "AUTEC conducts underwater testing and research. It's about submarines and torpedoes—underwater vessels, not UFOs."

Rob shot back: "When was the last time that the Navy shot a torpedo at an enemy vessel—the Korean War?"

Now Commander Richard laughed. "There's more to AUTEC than testing torpedoes. Far more."

~~~~~

On our third day in Andros, our interviews completed, we prepared to return to West Palm Beach. Because I had flown over the base with the Discovery Channel years earlier, I decided to do so again as we headed back. That was probably a mistake. When we took off, the closest islands—Nassau, the Berry Islands, and Freeport—were visible on the moving map screen. My plane had a state-of-art glass panel, the Garmin G-1000, an avionics device that makes flight information easier to scan and process. We could see the vast reaches of ocean interspersed with named islands.

But as I flew over the base for a quick look at the facility, the plane's moving map screen went blank. Although satellites sometimes have temporary glitches and reception disappears, it's highly unusual for the land masses to vanish completely from the moving map. All 700 islands of the Bahamas were simply gone; 5,382 square miles of the Atlantic dotted with lands were suddenly reduced to nothing but ocean.

Fortunately, the weather was clear and I was familiar enough with the route to follow the chain of Berry Islands and use them as visual cues to find my way to Freeport. From there, we headed directly west. The moving map screen remained blank the entire trip back. As soon as we reached the mainland, the screen lit up. I had the GPS tested the next morning, and was told that it was functioning perfectly. So what happened?

Maybe the Cessna's loss of the moving map was simply a random glitch in a new piece of equipment. But considering that we didn't ask permission to fly over the base and therefore probably violated airspace restrictions, our action could have triggered a reaction. When Rob related this story to former AUTEC employee David Malcolm, he laughed and replied, "They zapped you. You were a target of opportunity."

Chapter
10

Space-Time Warps

Wouldn't it be great if we could teleport ourselves to our destinations when we're stuck in traffic? Or how about avoiding long TSA lines at the airport or crowded airplanes? A snap of the finger and you're there, wherever you want to go. Is that just a fantasy? Or could teleportation—also known as linear displacement—be real?

I think it happens. It happened to me. However, I wouldn't want it to happen again, at least not in such a harrowing way. But I'm not the only one who has had these experiences.

Teleportation is defined as the transfer of matter or energy from one point to another without traversing the physical space between them. My father, his business partner, and I had literally jumped 90 miles in the midst of a dangerous electrical storm in our extraordinary flight in 1970. We arrived 30 minutes early with extra gas that should have been burned on the flight. That meant we had breached the space-time continuum.

I would later find out others had experienced a similar shift in time and space. In Chapter 9, I related the story of the AUTEC employee who approached me in West Palm Beach restaurant who described an experience in which a submarine instantly shifted 100 miles in the Tongue of the Ocean. That was one of many stories I have collected involving teleportation. A number of them took place on land and were detailed in Chapter 7. These experiences might be more common than we imagine.

Space-Time Continuum

Ever since Albert Einstein announced his special theory of relativity, time has been linked to space. We're all familiar with the three dimensions: up and down, side to side, and forward and back. Time is the fourth dimension and, as such, takes on a geometric quality. This new entity is called the space-time continuum. It's a continuum because the three dimensions of space are infinite and the duration of time is endless—or so it is perceived by quantum physics.

Space-time doesn't evolve. It just exists. Physicists consider our world embedded in the space-time continuum, and all events, places, moments in history, and actions of any sort are described in terms of their location in space-time. Interestingly, time travel is possible as a result of Einstein's theory. If you were able to move close to the speed of light in a space ship, time aboard the ship would move slower than time on Earth. So although time moves at a certain pace on Earth, you could take a round-trip tour through the galaxy and return to find your friends had aged much faster than you. Essentially, upon your return you would find that you had traveled to the future.

Now here's where teleportation fits in. Einstein and physicist Nathan Ryan used the theory of relativity to prove the existence of bridges through space-time. These bridges are known as wormholes, and provide shortcuts through space. Mass and gravity bend space so that the universe is curved. Wormholes bore through the curving or folded universe so that moving from one end of a wormhole to another is a shorter distance than following the curved surface.

Look at it this way: Imagine part of the universe as U-shaped. To get from the top of one side to the top of the other would require going down one side, then up the other. But a wormhole would go directly across the top of the U, a much shorter distance, resulting in a leap of space and time.

Now think of the top of either side of the U as stars. Following a wormhole through the fabric of space and time would result in a journey from one star to the other, possibly moving faster than the speed of light. If you were recording time on the journey through the wormhole, it might take six months. But when you arrived at your destination, you might find that years had passed. So the space warp allowed you to jump ahead in both space and time.

Professor John Wheeler of Princeton University created the term "wormhole" to describe these mini black holes or "transit tunnels" across time and space. He explained that they are constantly blinking in and out all around us. In other words, they exist for only a limited time.

However, scientists tell us that traveling through a wormhole could result in radiation exposure, dangerous contact with exotic matter, and the possible collapse of the wormhole. Ouch!

Right now our knowledge of how to prevent such calamities is limited, but keep in mind that when rail travel was developed with the steam engine in the early 1800s, some scientists thought it was a dangerous development. For example, Dr. Dionysys of University College London said: "Rail travel at high speed is not possible because passengers, unable to breathe, would die of asphyxia." President Martin Van Buren believed that "the Almighty certainly never intended that people should travel at such breakneck speed," referring to the current limit of 15 miles per hour. As time went on, people continued to believe that travel at more than 15 miles, 35 miles, and 50 miles per hour would snatch the breath out of passenger's lungs and even peel off their faces. Yikes!

From a more cosmic perspective, we could be in a similar situation regarding wormholes. Many scientists aren't convinced that wormholes exist, but if they do, traveling in one would be a perilous journey. Meanwhile, some people—including myself—believe that we have inadvertently traveled through either wormholes or warp bubbles, and survived. (Much more on warp bubbles in the next chapter.)

If I were to say that I had actually seen a rip in the fabric of the space-time continuum when I flew through the tunnel vortex, it might sound crazy. Yet, that is what scientists at the Laser Interferometer Gravitational-Wave Observatory said they observed in February 2016 when they detected gravitational waves. That means they observed tiny ripples in the fabric of space and time, something that Einstein predicted a century ago. What I saw on the inside of the tunnel vortex could very well have been ripples forming in the space-time continuum that would send me 90 miles in an instant.

But of course I'm not the only pilot who has had astonishing experiences that appear related to electronic fog and breaches in the space-time continuum.

A Time Freeze

John R. Hawke may be the only pilot who experienced not one, but two breaches of the space-time continuum. He spent years in the Royal Air Force and had flown over all the world's oceans. He also instructed aerobatics in the double-supersonic English Electric Lightning jet fighter. A tall, broad-shouldered athletic man, he was once the heavyweight boxing champion of the Royal Air Force.

Hawke could fly just about anything. He performed in many air shows with pilot/author Martin Caidin, and they became friends. Caidin wrote about Hawke's two incidents involving time distortions in *Ghost of the Air: True Stories of Aerial Hauntings.* Caidin is vague about dates, either because Hawke never told him when the incidents occurred, or it didn't matter to Caidin as much as the specifics about the airplanes and the details of the flights. From other references, it seems the incidents took place in the 1960s. Both pilots are now deceased, so there is no way to verify these stories. But if Caidin ever doubted the veracity of Hawke's recollections, he gave no such indication in his comments.

The first incident is a case of missing time. It occurred when Hawke was flying a Riley Dove from Miami to Bermuda. About halfway to his destination, he became enveloped in a glassy, yellow mist. He couldn't see the horizon or the ocean. It was probably similar to the electronic fog that I encountered. Hawke was a skilled pilot and was confident that he could continue to fly on the proper heading to Bermuda by using his instruments to navigate. However, after flying in the mist for three hours, the estimated time to reach Bermuda, he was still in it and unable to see land or water.

Hawke forged ahead, flying on and on for another five hours until he finally broke free of the mist. He squinted as he flew into bright sunlight and was astonished to see that Bermuda was directly in front of him. He contacted the airport tower and made a normal landing. It took him five hours longer than expected—but that wasn't all.

After landing, Hawke refueled the plane because the tanks should have been near empty after the lengthy flight. He was amazed to find out that he had landed with about a hundred gallons of gas. That was just about what he had estimated would be left in the tanks for the normal three-hour flight. However, he had flown an unexpected additional five hours and the engine should have consumed all the extra gas.

In my case, I ended up with 10 extra gallons of fuel. Whereas Hawke arrived five hours late with extra fuel, I landed half an hour early. Had I flown into the near future and Hawke back in time?

Caidin wrote in his book that Hawke had no idea how it could be possible not to burn the fuel. "That bloody machine gave us five extra hours of flying and, according to the fuel in the tanks, which I personally checked after landing, it didn't consume a drop of fuel for all that time."

The only way Hawke could fly for five hours and not burn any fuel would be if five hours passed for Hawke, but not for the airplane. It sounds like a case of missing time. Where was Hawke for those five hours? Time must have distorted for him when he entered the electronic fog. It was as if he had become trapped in a wormhole, and space and time had frozen for five hours. Maybe he was simply stuck in the same moment and the same location in the space-time continuum for five hours. Or maybe he was in a time loop, moving back in time in the same space, then moving ahead in time, then circling back again. Five hours passed and he never made any headway until he finally broke out of the fog.

I was in the fog for only a few minutes, but traveled an impossible distance. Hawke was in the fog for a long time, but traveled only a short distance, or no distance at all. Space-time warped or froze for Hawke. So he and I experienced a distortion of the space-time continuum, but in different ways. It seemed that Hawke experienced time travel to the near past over and over again.

Before getting into Hawke's second experience, let's take a closer look at the concept of time travel to the past.

Time Travel

In the classic novel *The Time Machine* by H.G. Wells, the protagonist settles into a special chair with blinking lights, spins a few dials, and instantly arrives several hundred thousand years into the future. England has long ago disappeared and is now a land inhabited by strange creatures called Morlocks and Eloi.

In *Timeline*, a 1999 novel by Michael Crichton, several of the characters are sent back to the Middle Ages in a time machine. Time travelers are pushed through wormholes, but to survive the process, the subjects are disassembled into "quantum foam," a basic unit of matter within subatomic particles, then reassembled at their destination in time and space.

When Carl Sagan wrote his novel *Contact,* he consulted his friend Kip Thorne for technical help on time travel. Thorne, a relativity expert at the California Institute of Technology, suggested that Sagan use a wormhole for time travel rather than a black hole. He reasoned that a wormhole would allow a time traveler to actually go somewhere, whereas a black hole is a one-way journey to nowhere. Thorne's idea not only gave Sagan's story more credibility, but led to a half dozen scientific papers on time travel.

In recent years, time travel has been gaining the attention not only of novelists and mystics, but also among scientists. Remarkable advances in quantum gravity are reviving the theory. Theoretical physicists now say that the theory of wormholes actually could offer a means to support time travel.

In June 2014, scientists at the University of Queensland in Australia demonstrated that one photon can pass through a wormhole and interact with its older self—in other words, travel back in time. Their research was published in *Nature Communications* in a study entitled "Experimental Simulation of Closed Timelike Curves." An article in the online journal *Collective Evolution* explains that this time travel experiment is related to "closed timelike curves," or CTC.

> CTCs are used to simulate extremely powerful gravitational fields, like the ones produced by a spinning black hole, and could, theoretically (based on Einstein's theory of general relativity), warp the fabric of existence so that space-time bends back on itself—thus creating a CTC, almost like a path that could be used to travel back in time.

According to an article in *Scientific American,* time travel to the past should be possible based on Einstein's theory of general relativity, which describes gravity as the warping of space-time by energy and matter. A strong gravitational pull created by a black hole could warp the fabric of existence so that space-time bends back on itself. That would create a "closed time-like curve," a loop that could be traversed to travel back in time. That sounds a lot like Hawke's experience, but that wasn't the only instance in which he encountered a crack in the space-time continuum.

A Leap Ahead

John Hawke's second mysterious experience is a truly strange case, as detailed in Caidin's book *Ghosts of the Air*. It's possibly the most fascinating in-flight space-time warp account ever recorded. He was flying a twin-engine Piper Aztec from Fort Lauderdale to Bermuda. It was a delivery flight and one that he didn't think would be a challenge. "It was just a jump across some water. Nice little trip," he later recalled.

He was told to expect puffy cumulus clouds between 4,000 and 8,000 feet. If he wanted to fly higher, he would find a helpful tailwind at 11,000 feet.

Quoted by Caidin in *Ghosts of the Air,* he described the situation.

I was on auto-pilot, everything neat as a pin, and I'd crossed the drink a few hundred times already. It was like being at home. Everything was perfect until I found myself staring at the mag compass. I was staring at it all right, but I couldn't see the stupid thing.

The compass card was spinning so fast that it was a blur and suddenly Hawke started feeling woozy. He was losing his sense of balance and his peripheral vision began to darken. "I'm accustomed to gray-outs when high G-forces begin to dim your vision along the edges. But this time there weren't any G-forces involved, and I had that instinctive certainty that I was very likely to pass out."

Now his expertise came into play. He was already flying on auto-pilot, but that wasn't good enough. Instantly, he pushed his seat back as far as it would go. If he was going to pass out, he wasn't going to fall on the yoke. That would send the plane into a tailspin. Before he could do anything else, he felt himself losing strength. He leaned back against the headrest and looked up through the windshield. All he saw was a creamy yellow fog. No clouds, no water, no horizon, no blue. The last thing he did before losing consciousness was look at his watch. "My arm felt like lead, but I fixed the numbers in my head, and the lights went out."

He awoke 59 minutes later. If the gauges were to be trusted, he was still flying northeast. Now he could see the sun and realized that the gauges were accurate. He felt drained, but otherwise okay. "I looked up and there was a lovely contrail. Just beautiful. Got on the horn right off and gave them a call. I told them I was under them, and asked where in the devil I was."

Hawke was astonished by what they told him. At first he didn't believe it. He was 400 miles from where he had been just an hour before. His plane's maximum speed was about 180 miles an hour, but he was cruising at a much slower speed. But in that hour, he had covered more than twice the distance that the plane could travel in that time. He turned due west and landed in Virginia.

I estimate that the time-space distortion Hawke encountered in the electronic fog moved him ahead an hour 52 minutes and 220 miles too far during the hour he spent in the fog. It was impossible, of course. Yet, when a pilot is trapped in electronic fog, time can distort and the seemingly impossible can happen.

After reading about Hawke's experience, I realized that I might have passed through a breach in the space-time continuum—the core of Einstein's special theory of relativity—on my flight. Just as scientists at the University of Queensland sent an elementary particle—a photon—back in time, physicists also have been able to send tiny particles called muons, which are similar to electrons, forward in time by manipulating the gravity around them.

Wormholes are both natural—relics of the Big Bang—and man-made, created by particle accelerators. If a way were found to stabilize and expand artificial wormholes, controlled time travel would be possible. But some researchers think that nature might already be doing the trick, just as nature started fires before humans learned to control fire.

Magnetic Vortices

Dr. Michael Preisinger, a German historian and scuba diving instructor, recorded locations of magnetic anomalies in the Bermuda Triangle and theorizes they are related to micro-wormholes. He didn't believe the stories about the Bermuda Triangle until his company sent him on a six-month stint in Nassau, Bahamas. His task was to develop a tourist program for scuba divers and assist German tourists. But when he kept hearing reports from boaters who had experienced spinning compasses or sudden deviations in their compass readings, he became curious.

"My curiosity as a historian got the better of me. I decided to look for magnetic field anomalies in the places where the deviations had been noted, and tried to bring back exact figures for those deviations," he wrote in his book, *Das Bermuda-Rätsel Gelöst* (*The Bermuda Riddle Solved*).

He showed scientists his figures and they conceded that the deviations could be the result of brief appearances of micro-wormholes. Among those scientists mentioned on Preisinger's website was Grazyna Fosar, a physicist from Berlin. Preisinger wrote that Fosar joined him on a radio show and said: "From the physicist's point of view, gates to hyperspace can be the only reasonable explanation for these mysterious deviations."

Preisinger also noted on his site that Professor Tsung-Min Gung, a physicist from Tokyo, told him that such deviations might be a way of locating wormholes. "If the theories of inter-dimensional connections are not completely wrong, and can develop in the way I am expecting them to, the strong interdependencies with gravitation and the Earth's magnetic field may be a way to track them down."

Considering that wormholes could be "transit tunnels" between dimensions of reality, it's not surprising that UFOs and USOs are so closely associated with the Bermuda Triangle and other areas where magnetic field anomalies have been reported. I also wonder if it was mere coincidence that the AUTEC base on Andros Island was located in the midst of these magnetic deviations. It could be that the secret part of the base's projects deal with these anomalies and related phenomena.

I'll close this chapter with a quote about wormholes by renowned cosmologist and physicist Stephen Hawking. It's from a lecture called "Space and Time Warps" that he gave on October 18, 1995.

> Closely related to time travel, is the ability to travel rapidly from one position in space, to another. As I said earlier, Einstein showed that it would take an infinite amount of rocket power, to accelerate a space ship to beyond the speed of light. So the only way to get from one side of the galaxy to the other, in a reasonable time, would seem to be if we could warp space-time so much that we created a little tube or wormhole. . . . Such wormholes have been seriously suggested, as being within the capabilities of a future civilization.

Chapter
11

Building a Warp Drive

It happened so many times that I had come to expect it. I would tell my story on a cable channel documentary and immediately afterward a scientist would appear to contest it. I might have flown through a tunnel between two thunderstorms, they said, but I didn't breach the space-time continuum and leap ahead 90 miles. I was wrong about that, because that was impossible.

Then I met David Pares, a former Air Force meteorologist who teaches physics, meteorology, and astronomy at the University of Nebraska and other colleges in that area. He was fascinated by my story and wanted to know more. I soon learned that David was not an ordinary scientist. He was building a warp drive—as in the power behind the USS *Enterprise* in *Star Trek*—and he was doing it in his garage. But before taking a closer look at his work on the frontier of science, let's go back to what originally motivated him to pursue such a mind-boggling project.

Unlike the vast majority of his colleagues, David Pares accepts the reality of UFOs as crafts from elsewhere. In fact, he had seen one when he was a teenager and it changed his life.

It was a cool, clear-blue morning sky in late August of 1969 when it happened. David Pares was 16 years old and waiting with five friends to go to swim class at Goodyear Lake near Oneonta, New York, when he saw a silver metallic disk moving across the sky.

Apollo 11 had just landed on the moon a month prior, the country was upbeat on the space program, and David and his friends were going to go to the moon and beyond the first chance they got. And now this—a UFO.

The intriguing thing about this sighting was that it coincided with another one that happened just 10 hours before David's encounter. The local news reported that several children in the Unadilla area in upstate New York had stumbled upon a landed silver flying saucer while playing in the woods and ran home terrified.

The report detailed that the children told their parents that when they had approached the craft, they saw people wearing silver-colored suits nearby. One of them spotted the children and started to run toward them. That's when the kids ran off. The parents called the authorities, who subsequently investigated the clearing, and found several uniform depressions in the ground.

After David heard the story, he had a good laugh. He didn't believe a word of it, nor did he believe UFOs even existed. His father offered the same opinion. The next day he and his friends met for the trip to swim class and David started to tell the guys about the ridiculous report from the previous night. Everyone was laughing about it when he noticed something out of the corner of his eye.

A silver metallic disk was just clearing the top of the nearby mountain. He pointed and shouted, "Look! Look! It's a flying saucer." He was transfixed by the sight. He shouted for someone to run in the house and get an adult out there to see it. Who would believe them otherwise?

The old saying, "What goes around, comes around," seemed to fit. He had been making fun of kids who saw UFOs, now he was seeing one. The vehicle had no windows, no hatch or panel outlines, protrusions, engines, smoke, or noises with one exception: A light air buffing sound could be heard as the craft moved overhead, similar to the sound of air against the canopy when flying in a glider. The disk was about 60 feet in diameter and about 10 to 12 feet in girth.

It was traveling at about 20 miles per hour and 500 feet above the terrain. It was moving right to left in front of them. The sun was behind them so they had a good view. The craft was extremely stable, and the symmetrical convex lens–shaped object had very distinctive edges.

As the craft passed in front of them, it banked about 15 degrees, revealing the entire topside. David sensed that it knew they were there and to this day his hair still bristles when he mentally replays the encounter. Even more intriguing was that when it banked the sun illuminated very subtle striation patterns in the metal surface, which ran from the front of the leading edge over the center girth to the back of the craft.

This view made it clear that the craft did not rotate and that it appeared to have a front and back, even though it had a symmetrical disk shape. David noticed that the craft didn't lose any altitude, in spite of its slow speed and angular position. He has never seen any aircraft have this incredible stability and impeccable maneuvering capability at such a low speed. A Piper cub stalls at 38 miles per hour.

After the craft passed by, it quickly leveled out, and rapidly accelerated. They tracked it across the lake and valley floor to the next rise some 10 miles away. The mother of one of his friends came out, but she couldn't spot it as they tried to point it out in the sky. They ended up skipping the swim class and talking about what we had seen. Later, he excitedly told his parents.

"My father told me, 'Oh for God's sake! You didn't see anything. What! Are you crazy? Now look you better not tell anybody about this. What would people think? You don't want people putting a label on you? Do you?'"

The encounter, Pares says, changed his life forever. He dropped out of extra-curricular activities during his senior year and took a new track. He kept thinking of the sighting and realized that there was a great probability that we are not alone. "I started to hone my skills in aviation, astronomy, and a host of fields in math, science, and engineering. It was 45 seconds that changed my life."

The Connection

In a single week, I might receive emails from India, England, and Poland, all from people wanting to communicate with me about my experience in the Bermuda Triangle. The inquiries come from all over the world and most of them are from students working on a school project about the Bermuda Triangle. One day I received an email from a college student in Nebraska that was quite different from most inquiries. Instead of asking me questions, she had an idea for me.

She was taking a physics course at the College of Saint Mary from Professor David Pares. It seems that Pares was quite interested in the Bermuda Triangle and in my theory about electronic fog. Her idea was for me to get together with Pares. Apparently he was a little shy and he didn't think he should bother me.

She sent me his résumé and I was impressed. She arranged for us to talk and that phone conversation was the beginning of many communications. I found that he was quite knowledgeable about the Bermuda Triangle, especially regarding meteorology. When the History Channel contacted me to do another documentary, I asked the producer if David Pares could play a major role; at the last minute they agreed. I called David and he was on a plane a couple of days later. We flew into the Bermuda Triangle with the documentary film crew the next day. Since that first documentary, David has also appeared with me on Bermuda Triangle productions by the Discovery Channel and the BBC.

When David and I met for the first time in person, an interesting thing happened. While we were discussing my Bermuda Triangle experience, he asked me numerous questions about the event and I could see he was trying to picture it in his mind. I told him I must have been traveling at least 2,000 miles per hour while I was in the electronic fog in order to reach Miami Beach in three minutes. He disagreed and said I was probably flying at my indicated airspeed of 180 miles per hour. What happened was that when we came out of the tunnel vortex and the electronic fog attached to the plane, we were 10 miles offshore of Miami and then it took me three minutes to reach Miami Beach as the electronic fog dissipated.

My first reaction to his theory was "No way." When I came out of the tunnel, I estimated we were 90 miles east of Miami, not 10 miles east. After mulling it over for several months, my thinking changed. He could be right. Maybe it was like going through a wormhole and that is why I felt that strange sensation of zero gravity combined with hydroplaning while this was happening. Pares thinks I had a "linear displacement"—he prefers that phrase to teleportation—of 80 miles in a matter of seconds, perhaps even a fraction of a second.

Most of us, upon seeing a UFO, would wonder who was driving the vehicle and where it came from. But the dominant question for Pares was: What was the vehicle's means of propulsion?

As he pursued his career as a meteorologist and a college instructor, the idea of building a warp drive was a dream he pondered on and tinkered with among students and friends. However, when he saw a documentary in which I talked about my flight through the tunnel vortex, he realized that I might hold the key not only to the Bermuda Triangle phenomenon, but also to the development of a warp drive. When I flew between the two thunderstorm clouds and leaped in space from near Bimini to Miami Beach, Pares suspected that I must have flown into a naturally occurring warp bubble generated by the intense electrical forces in the heart of the storm.

For two years, he watched the documentaries I appeared on and studied my flight in detail from the point of view of a scientist. In doing so, he presented a new perspective on my experience. "The magnetic tri-pole field within the thunderstorm created a local space warp bubble around the craft that compressed the fabric of space," he explained. He added that the warp bubble contained enough energy to move the plane in a straight line close to 100 miles in one second. That's the equivalent of 360,000 miles per hour. The reason the plane and passengers weren't blown apart into thousands of pieces is what makes warp drive travel unique. My plane didn't move from one place to another in the normal sense. Instead, the space in front of the plane contracted instantly and shifted the Bonanza to another location.

David Pares building a space warp drive in his garage. Photo credit: Nancy Pares.

Inside David Pares's garage lab where he is building the famed engine of science fiction. Photo credit: David Pares.

Working in his garage workshop, Pares is convinced that he has demonstrated a way to compress space. To do so, he has duplicated—on a small scale—a tri-pole electrical field and sent a laser beam through the center of it, projecting the beam onto a screen. The image on the screen seems to indicate that the beam is being compressed. He explains that it should be impossible to maneuver the beam in such a manner. The only way to accomplish such a feat would be to compress space—the key to creating a warp drive engine.

Theoretical physicists believe that enormous amounts of energy is required to create a warp bubble, but Pares says he can do it with a couple hundred watts. By directing that low power through their array of custom-built, fractal patterned, V-shaped warp circuits, Pares and his team consistently documented the movement of a three-and-a-half pound weight in a Faraday cage (a container that blocks electromagnetic signals). Pares notes that it doesn't matter whether or not the object is magnetic. In principle, that shouldn't happen.

One of the models Pares has created that one day could fly without a gas engine or a battery—but with a warp drive. Photo credit: David Pares.

Pares's efforts to build a warp drive were influenced by Mexican physicist Miguel Alcubierre, who derived the physics that make a warp drive possible. Alcubierre's drive compresses space in front of a vehicle and expands it behind the craft. Where Pares parts from Alcubierre's warp drive concept is that he's convinced that a warp bubble does not require massive amounts of energy. He bluntly maintains: "You can create a warp bubble with less than five watts of energy."

The history of science and technology reveals that many inventions and advancements have taken place outside of standard laboratories. Charles Martin Hall, the son of a minister, was working in a woodshed laboratory in Ohio in 1886, and Paul Heroult was using a corner of his father's tannery in Paris in the same year when they both found a way to make aluminum a viable commercial product. I like to compare the idea of David Pares building a warp drive in his garage to Steve Jobs, who once built computers in his garage. And I'm not the only one who sees the potential of his work.

In an article for *Motherboard,* an online science-tech magazine, writer Doug Bierend said, "Who knows, maybe the precursor to humanity's future among the stars does begin in a garage in Omaha. . . . If Pares's claims are true, it'll take a demonstration of sufficient clarity to leave no one in doubt."

As Bierend points out in the article entitled "That Physicist in Omaha Is Still Working on a Warp Drive in his Garage," mainstream scientists are hesitant to embrace Pares's claim that he has created a warp bubble in his garage. They want to see his research published in a science journal before they take him seriously. Without such an endorsement, grant money to expand his research remains out of reach. So far, his efforts to gain acceptance from the scientific establishment and physicists in high-end laboratories have met with rejection. When he submitted a paper to a symposium for advanced spacecraft engine design, it was turned down.

An article, "Is Warp Drive Real," published March 10, 2015, on the NASA website, concisely states the current paradigm. Marc Mills, a former NASA Glen physicist, writes that warp drive—faster-than-light travel—remains speculation. "The bulk of scientific knowledge concludes that it's impossible, especially when considering Einstein's Theory of Relativity."

According to that theory, it takes an infinite amount of energy to accelerate an object with mass up to the speed of light. Therefore, it would appear that having a spacecraft exceeding the speed of light would be impossible. However, Pares points out that our current understanding of physics leaves open the possibility of *space itself* traveling at or beyond the speed of light. In other words, the actual fabric of the universe moves, taking the craft along with it.

"There are certainly some credible concepts in scientific literature, however it's too soon to know if they are viable." Mills adds, "There are many 'absurd' theories that have become reality over the years of scientific research. But for the near future, warp drive remains a dream."

Besides the barrier of incredulity, Pares's interest in the Bermuda Triangle and UFOs doesn't win him any favors from mainstream science. Pares is also the faculty advisory for the Mutual UFO Network (MUFON) student organization.

But he remains undeterred by the lack of institutional recognition. In fact, he noted that his UFO experience was what pushed him to the sciences. He wanted to study as many disciplines as possible, because he realized they were all interconnected. He told *Motherboard:* "If I were just in the physics discipline, I would have never figured this out. It would've meant sticking with chemical rocketry, maybe getting into ion drives. But if you get into this exotic stuff, you're going to be labeled as a weirdo, as an outcast."

You can hear the frustration in his voice when he talks about being seen as an outsider tinkering in his garage. That narrow concept of what constitutes genuine scientific research means that scientists in the big labs won't even bother challenging the conclusions he's reached.

Although I'm not a scientist, I understand David's situation regarding the scientific community. For years, scientists have dismissed electronic fog as if it was something that existed only in my imagination. They had never heard of it so it couldn't be real. After all, I was a pilot, not a meteorologist. Pilots fly through fog. Fog does not attach itself to airplanes like Velcro.

Pares, the former Air Force meteorologist, has a more open interpretation of what I've experienced. He recognizes a "fog" can indeed attach to an airplane and travel with it, that it can be a precursor to the appearance of a warp bubble. He notes that the term "electronic fog" is my creation, essentially my brand, and he accepts it. He explains electronic fog this way: "It's ionized energy in clouds embedded in a dipole field that forms a cocoon around the planes." Evidence of the dipole field is seen in cases such as mine and the flight described by Martin Caidin in Chapter 6, in which there is a hole in the cloud below or above the plane, or both, that travels with the plane as it seemingly flies through fog.

Applying Science to the Mystery

The title reads *Science Behind Bruce Gernon's Flight 4 December 1970*. It's a detailed 23-page report with charts, graphs, and photos accompanying the text. David Pares closely examined my encounter with the Bermuda Triangle phenomenon then applied his knowledge of meteorology and physics.

He began by doing the math. What was the distance of the flight? How long did it take? What kind of airplane was I flying? What was the fuel capacity? How many gallons of fuel were typically used on a flight between West Palm Beach and Andros Island?

He noted that to travel a distance of 250 miles in 47 minutes would require flying at 319.14 miles per hour. But then he pointed out that specifications for a 1970 Beechcraft Bonanza is a cruising speed of 190 mph and never to exceed 234 mph. In other words, my plane should have broken apart if I traveled that distance at that speed. But the plane held together.

He also applied his meteorological background and studied the weather between Andros Island and Miami Beach on December 4, 1970. He said that by late afternoon unstable air existed along the flight route that could generate thunderstorms, a scenario that usually exists between high and low pressure systems over Florida and the waters off-shore. He wrote, "These are the major contributing factors in setting up the electrical conduits and connectivity for electronic fog generation and in Bruce's particular flight the possibility of the warping of space."

Pares went on to describe the power of a mega electric thunder-storms like the ones that I was trapped in on that flight. Whereas typical thunderstorms generate between 100,000 to 200,000 volts per meter, mega electric thunderstorms can exceed 400,000 volts per meter and a current of more than 200,000 amps. That potentially is more pow-erful than a small atomic bomb. "This would create a powerful conduit of energy between the magnetosphere, thermosphere, ionosphere, and the ground. The total energy flux from space would be in the terra watts of energy." Pares points out that thunderstorms also produce anti-matter that provide additional energy in the cloud formation.

Student pilots are typically told to avoid flying into "sucker holes" between storm clouds. David's description of the power in those storms provides strong support of that piece of advice. He goes on to explain in his report how that power can generate a warp bubble. "It is this situation that induced the thunderstorms and caused a warping or compression in the fabric of space around Bruce Gernon's aircraft as he entered his only escape route, the hole in the clouds."

Besides compressing space, Pares points out that the power within the thunderclouds also creates the electrical energy to ionize the surrounding air and create conditions known as electronic fog. He explains that ionized particles are attracted to the carbon emissions of the aircraft engine so that the fog literally clings to the craft. Once the electronic fog surrounds an airplane, the pilot becomes locked in a dangerous situation.

According to Pares, based on where I entered the cloud at 10,000 feet, the frequencies of the fields with the cloud would have been somewhere between the 400 and 700 MHz range. That figure is based on his research and the flight Pares and I took on February 14, 2009. He said this would explain the electronic instruments going off-line, but not shutting down the engine due to the additional shielding in the engine compartment. This also explains why my radio still worked, because it was located in the instrument panel and therefore shielded by the surrounding instruments.

Pares also pointed out in his report that I entered the cloud tunnel at 10,000 feet and when I appeared near Miami Beach I was also at 10,000 feet.

The point here is that if this is a real example of a local space warp metric, it followed the curvature of the Earth. The warp metric appears to be influenced by mass. If we could artificially induce this situation one could travel vast distances on the earth in just a few seconds and still maintain flight levels for separation from commercial traffic. Obviously, the potential for space travel also has some real possibilities here as well.

Pares was also intrigued by the fact that my plane was lost from radar, but I still had radio contact with Miami. He noted that by following the rules of relativity, the movement of my plane through the last 100 miles would have ripped the craft apart. "That's why we are looking at a localized warping of space created by the energy of the surrounding clouds that blocked his flight path and the opposing weaker energy field (the cloud tunnel) which he flew into creating a local flat space warp bubble containment field."

Astonishingly, he calculated that I flew 90 miles in about one second, then 10 miles over the next three minutes with the electronic fog surrounding the plane and breaking up as I approached land. Yet during that near-instantaneous 90-mile shift that he calls a "linear displacement," my plane essentially was not moving.

He explains that in a warp bubble the space is moved with no effect on the object.

Also, while in transit, the on-board clock runs at the same speed as the clock of an external observer. The crew of the airplane would not have experienced any acceleration of g-forces once inside the field. This may explain why he could use the radio since the transit was only a linear displacement and time dilation was not a consideration.

Because the warp bubble theory doesn't follow Einstein's laws of relativity, Pares maintained that no shift in time occurred. That may be true, but I did arrive 30 minutes earlier than was possible on a flight of that distance. Normally, a 250-mile flight in a Bonanza from 1970 would take 75 minutes. My flight lasted 45 minutes. I also ended up with 10 extra gallons of fuel that should have been used. To me, that seemed like time travel.

Pares also explains that while I was inside the warp bubble, the plane vanished from radar. When the tower finally located me, I was near Miami Beach but believed I was more than 80 miles from Miami. Pares figures they lost me at the first 15-second sweep of the radar as I exited the cloud and then picked me up on the next sweep of the Miami radar antenna, which then put me over Miami Beach.

I am particularly impressed and pleased with what Pares concludes in his report about my flight. "This could be the first real documented case of a natural warping of the fabric of space and an external ionized confinement field (electronic fog) around an aircraft produced from mega electrical thunderstorm activity."

~~~~~

David Pares is building one of the most exotic engines ever created. I feel greatly honored to have played a key role in his research. Hopefully, David and others who follow him will be able to turn the engine of science fiction into the planet-hopping warp drive of the future. If I've contributed to that happening, as David attests, it makes all my efforts to tell the world about my flight through the Bermuda Triangle well worthwhile.

Chapter
12

Remote Viewing the Triangle

Now for something really strange.

I want to talk about a matter I've never revealed in any of the documentaries, or in our earlier book, *THE FOG*. It's about how a former well-known psychic spy for the Army and CIA used his talents to explore aspects of my story and the Bermuda Triangle in general. But first, some background.

In 1970, Prentice Hall published *Psychic Discoveries Behind the Iron Curtain*, by Sheila Ostrander and Lynn Schroeder. The book apparently created enough of a stir within intelligence circles so that certain steps were taken. According to *remoteviewed.com*, one of these steps occurred in 1973 when the Rand Corporation was hired to determine if paranormal phenomena existed, how the Russians were investigating it, and how this compared with American efforts.

The 33-page report covered the nature of paranormal phenomena, possible military applications, and the differences between research in the two countries. The study concluded that although American researchers were dabbling, the Russians were involved in efforts to control and apply psychic powers for the benefit of the state.

As a result, from 1972 to 1995, more than $20 million was pumped into research that led to a secret government program involving psychic spying. Once known as clairvoyance, the ability to "see" at a distance became known as "remote viewing" when it became a controlled process under the auspices of the military. Most of the targets dealt with defense and national security issues, and involved psychically spying on enemies. Remarkably, the targets were placed in sealed envelopes with only a multiple-digit number written on the outside.

One of the top performers was Joe McMoneagle, a retired chief warrant officer, United States Army, and was Remote Viewer #001 in the military's secret program known as "Stargate" for 19 years. He has authored four books on remote viewing and has had two research papers published in scientific journals on the same subject.

Rob MacGregor, my coauthor, is an acquaintance of McMoneagle and asked him to remote view four targets related to the Bermuda Triangle: my flight into the electronic fog, my UFO experience one month later, Flight 19, and AUTEC, the Navy base on Andros Island where my flight began.

The targets were provided to his monitor, Nancy McMoneagle, who is Joe's wife and president and executive director of the Monroe Institute, an organization that studies out-of-body experiences.

When Joe begins a session, he moves into a deeply relaxed state, similar to meditation, by taking several deep breaths and releasing distracting thoughts. "The idea behind meditation is that when one sits passively and attempts to silence the inner fires of activity, deeper thoughts and resources become apparent and surface," McMoneagle wrote in *Remote Viewing Secrets*. "All you have to do is change 'deeper thoughts and resources' to 'information' and you have a near perfect definition of the act of remote viewing."

Inside the sealed envelope of Target #1, unknown to McMoneagle, was an illustration of my Beechcraft Bonanza entering the tunnel in the massive storm cloud and into the electronic fog. He was only given brief instructions, which were written on the outside of the envelope. What follows are the instructions and his written conclusions about the subject sealed in the envelope. The sessions were conducted in his home with Nancy McMoneagle serving as his monitor. After the four sessions were completed, Joe McMoneagle's reports were sent to us through the mail.

Please describe in detail the target on 12/4/1970:

Get a strong sense of noise, engine noise, or wind noise, and quick movement, as though moving in a vehicle of some kind. I'm sitting in the left hand seat, and I am male, and my hands are on a steering wheel that is shaped slightly funny. So, it is a different kind of car, maybe one of those radically different kinds of cars from back in the 70s. The interior seems to be radically different—laid out a bit strangely, longer curve to the interior roof, and the windows are different somehow.

I get a very strong sensation that I either know the driver or know something about the driver in some way, but there is also strangeness about that feeling as well. It's kind of a far off feeling about that as well—like an old but new feeling about that too. The driver is wearing some sort of headgear over his head, but it isn't a helmet. It might be some sort of headset for listening to music—stereo headsets for music. It might also be some sort of muffle to cut out the loud hissing sounds from the noise—I get a very strong sensation that there is a lot of loud engine or wind noise. Like the windows are open or something allowing for a lot of noise because of fast movement down the road.

The seats are strange as well, having a larger than usual console and what appears to be much more clutter between them. I get a feeling that it would be difficult to more around from seat to seat—like things have been jammed in some way between the seats. The dash panel also seems to be severely cluttered with a lot more equipment than the average automobile. There are many additional dials and radios than normal, as well as additional dials of some kind for the engine—apparently to monitor the engine. The radios appear to be quite important and the driver appears to be more concerned with the dash panel than watching where he is steering the automobile.

I'm getting a very strong feeling that the driver is turning equipment on and off rapidly, switching different things on and off, or changing from one switch to another. It's as if he's trying to reset or change many of the settings on the switches for some reason, like he is trying to correct some problem. The driver is quite agitated and upset with equipment, and seems unable to get it to reset properly.

I have a strong sensation that the loud hissing noises are coming from the headsets and he is trying to change channels on some of the radio equipment, but all he gets is overriding waves of white noise or static. Oceans of static or waves of static no matter what he come with the switches.

Interim Conclusion: This is 1970, so most of the electronics are electromagnetic, and most of the equipment is therefore physio-magnetic-based-electronics, which would indicate catastrophic system failure at a primary juncture within the system itself—hence the automobile can't or shouldn't be running. It is anyway, and the driver doesn't appear to be concerned with where he is going, but he does seem to be more concerned with the system failure. Therefore, it is highly unlikely that this is either an automobile or boat, and much more likely that it is an aircraft.

The problem appears to be a combination of a number of things, all falling within very narrow and precise parameters consistent with temperature and humidity (air/water) content constraints.

1. The sheet metal belly of the aircraft has attained a specific ambient temperature.
2. The sheet metal upper area of the aircraft has attained a specific ambient temperature.
3. The speed of the aircraft is a specific constant.
4. The aircraft has entered a very narrow channel of super calm air at a specific altitude which contains two very well defined temperature gradients that have slipstreamed together that are polar opposites to the variable temperatures of the aircraft skins (top and bottom).
5. As the aircraft passes through the grade-variant streams of air, they produce opposite magnetic charged air molecules to flow along with opposite sides of the aircraft skin.
6. These bi-polar discharges into the on-board grounds cause the on-board electronics to basically continually reset themselves in a set-loop that appears to be some sort of on-board jamming.

Believe the issue probably resolved itself for the pilot with a radical (scary) altitude change, maneuver, or course correction, or by flying out of the area where the well-defined temperature gradients existed—which were probably over land in conjunction with water, or coast line.

Joe McMoneagle initially seemed to think that he was remote viewing some kind of unusual car, but eventually pinpoints the vehicle as an aircraft. Although he never uses the words *fog* or *cloud*, his description of the conditions related to electromagnetic fields seems very much like electronic fog.

Flight 19

Target #2 was Flight 19. All he received from his monitor was a sealed envelope with these instructions on the outside:

1) Please describe target and... 2) describe details of event with target on date of interest and... 3) describe current location of target.

Inside the envelope was a folded piece of paper enclosed with the following description of the target: "U.S. Navy Flight 19—disappeared 12/5/1945."

In an email to us with the results in an attached file, Nancy McMoneagle noted: "He told me the other day as he worked on this target, 'Oh, I know what this is. . . . It's the missing flight that went down in the 40s near Florida.' You would think I'd get used to it, but he still amazes me!"

Here is what McMoneagle reported back to us in a written statement.

A description of Target (2) and their details (2) are:

Target appears to be a flight of aircraft, approximately three to possibly five aircraft sometimes flying in formation and sometimes breaking up to fly alone or some sort of separate stunts or acrobatically, (this occurred mostly at area indicated on map as the area where they "flew in circles.") There are other areas throughout the flight routes where other planes broke away to fly independent routes from the body large to apparently scout for land or objects in the water or for other unknown reasons at different times during the overall flight.

More specifically these aircraft are older, single-engine, rotary, prop-driven airplanes dating from approximately the mid-1940s. Dates of construction for the specific airplanes of interest appear to be specifically manufactured sometime between August and December of 1942, one aircraft having been constructed at a later time period June/July of 1943. The later manufactured aircraft had some modifications to it that were not made to the other aircraft, but they were not operating on the day of the flight due to the base of origin not having a mechanic with sufficient knowledge capable to enable sufficient repairs. These repairs were not considered major and would not have ground the aircraft in any event.

All of these aircraft were of WWII vintage, and appear to be medium short range bombers, probably ship/base bombers capable of both carrying torpedoes as well as heavy dive type bombs for shipping raids—this would make them Skyraider or Dauntless class type aircraft, given their wing shapes and body thicknesses. I would guess Dauntless, as I sense they had lower round entry holes in the lower fuselage areas, but I could be wrong. I also sense they could operated with three, but carried up to at least four men. Up top, and visible to the sky, were the pilot and co-pilot/gunner. Below, with a smaller window housed the navigator/bomber and the communications man. On this particular flight all planes were loaded as they were fulfilling their training requirements before leaves.

Description of events leading up to the loss of aircraft:

I believe the aircraft took off sometime in mid-day or afternoon as the sun was below peak. I believe it was Florida because it looks like Florida to me and I lived there all my life. (It's a place that is hard not to recognize—especially that coastline.)

The planes flew dead east at what appears to be top cruising speed which was approximately 340–360 mph, or that is what it feels like to me—given the smooth roll of the rotary engines. They have a very distinctive pitch when tuned to cruising speed—they were at approximately 5,000 feet, just above the lower clouds and in very clear open sky over smooth water, sunny day, with a light breeze.

They apparently flew due east to some very small islets and then broke up into pairs and did some acrobatic flying and dropped their bombs on some isolated piles of rocks in some out of the way area. It was some kind of a training exercise. It was very routine and very well executed. One of the aircraft stood off to one side flew a race track pattern to the southwest as this exercise was conducted. I believe this aircraft was stationed there to keep other aircraft out of the area as well as to warn boats that might appear to be wandering into the area. There were no mishaps of any kind. The entire exercise took approximately twelve minutes of flying time.

On terminating the exercise, the flight appeared to continue flying toward the east with a little bit of drift toward the north. They continued on this track for approximately eighteen minutes then executed a turn toward the north. They flew north (actually a little bit toward the west of north) for approximately fifteen minutes. At some point they began encountering heavy cloud cover over islands that were part of the Bahamas chain. At this point, they climbed to break free of the rough air conditions to approximately 8,000 feet, leveling out over heavy cloud cover. Once there they continued on their general northern direction for another five minutes. At this point, they realized they were missing a man from the formation.

They were able to contact the man by radio, but he could not find the rest of the flight. He was traveling generally north as well, but had not come out above the same level of cloud cover. Not finding the flight, he had dropped back down to the water and was now back on the deck under the clouds over water. He had turned around and was headed back toward the islands.

The flight leader then turned the entire flight around and headed them back toward the south to try and hook up with the man they had lost. He ordered the man to turn his aircraft around and fly north to meet them. In turning the flight around, they also dropped back to the deck. Flying back to the south, retracing their steps, they eventually did in fact retrace their steps (or so they thought) and met the aircraft they had become separated from, where he turned the entire group around once again and proceeded once again on their original heading north. What the group leader didn't know was they had drifted considerably west on the return as a result of prevailing winds, and the double-turns had confused them with regard to where they were in their flight plan.

My belief about what was actually happening here:

My sense is that between all the turning around and flying back and forth over islands, the men in all of the aircraft were becoming confused about where they were. All of these men, including the senior most man (flight leader) were not accustomed to the area they were flying in. Where they were normally accustomed to flying was between Key West and Miami. It is hard to imagine, but if you spend hundreds of hours doing the same thing over and over again, it becomes rote. Your body does things before your mind even thinks it. This becomes especially true with combat trained/experienced fliers. They are hardwired that way. It's part of the reason they survive. If they spent hundreds of hours training and flying over the Florida Keys, and then suddenly switched to the Bahama Islands it would be easy for them to become confused and disoriented—and that's what I sense is happening to them. Their minds superimposed the Florida Keys over the Bahamas.

As they flew north, they settled into a mindset that they were flying north to Miami!

Miami had to show up within a set time frame of flying—just like usual. Fifteen to twenty minutes. It didn't. They began to wonder why not. Someone got smart and decided they must be over the Bahamas. They turned for Florida—west. They flew for approximately fifteen minutes. But fuel began to concern them. What if it was wrong? Doubt set in. Maybe those islands they were over really were the Florida Keys, and all that flying had somehow gotten them back over the keys. If they kept flying due west, they'd end up going down in the middle of the Gulf of Mexico.

No one would find their bodies. Panic set in. They'd better turn around. At least they could find the islands maybe. They turned south again But, that can't be right either. More panic. Team leader knows by now that they are really in trouble. He no longer has a clue as to where they are. He is totally lost and up on the radio asking for help, but no one can hear them. They are too far away to be heard by anyone. He can't remember how many turns they've taken or where they came from. He knows the last two or three turns, so he knows he must at least take them back to their original flight path or at least as close as he can get them. He turns them back toward the north. It's their last turn, as they are nearly out of gas.

I believe they tighten up their formation and stick together until the end. They are scared and frightened, but there is little they can do. The continue to use their radios, but no one answers or responds. They make a pack. Then the first aircraft goes down, then they will fly the area until the all go down, each plane circling and staying on the radio until the last plane goes into the drink. It does no good. All planes go down, all planes are lost, as are all the men.

Additional Information:

I have a sense there is an additional plane that went down at approximately the same time. It was an Air Sea Rescue Aircraft. Twin-engine. Also rotary prop aircraft. Wing over pontoon type aircraft with five men on board, possibly carrying two extra men on that particular day as observers or search personnel. The search plane went down within 12 hours of the loss of the primary flight. The loss of the air and sea rescue flight, however, was not unusual, as the nature of the aircraft was not unknown to loss. During the war, it was renowned for its capacity to 'spontaneously combust' at time during a flight. Only the bravest men flew in it.

The flight went down off Melbourne, Florida. A little bit south, as indicated on attached map. I would also note that the combat aircraft are recoverable, as they are all in very deep water and probably not very deteriorated. However, it is my belief that the air and sea rescue aircraft probably exploded either prior to, or on impact and was scattered across a wide debris field. It appears to lie in approximately 650-700 feet of water and may be more difficult to find as a result of its shattered and less than superior condition.

The specifics that McMoneagle provided are impressive, and show that this type of target—military operations—were his forte during his years as Remote Viewer #001 for the Army. Of course, those targets were undoubtedly aimed at foreign military operations—especially the Russian military. Interestingly, he spent four and a half hours on this target, whereas he worked the other three each for an hour and a half.

A skeptic might say that once he figured out what the target was, he could have used his knowledge of the well-known "Lost Patrol" rather than any psychic abilities. The problem with that analysis—beyond the question of how he knew what the target was—is that McMoneagle's description of what happened includes elements that have never been reported. For instance, he says one of the planes was separated from the others, causing the other four to circle around looking for it. If that actually happened, it was never reported in any radio transmissions. Also, McMoneagle doesn't mention the problem reported by the lead pilot that his compass was malfunctioning. The fact that he doesn't mention it seems to indicate that McMoneagle wasn't working off a "fact sheet" on Flight 19, but was actually remote viewing the flight. Whether his conclusions were accurate or not is another matter.

McMoneagle's description confirms the issue of mental confusion, which he links to the numerous turns, and the lead pilot believing they were in the Florida Keys rather than the Bahamas. That conclusion fits well with the radio exchanges. He also says the planes all disappeared into the ocean somewhere off Melbourne, Florida. Interestingly, if his conclusion about the final destination is correct, it dismisses any paranormal outcome, such as the planes shifting into another dimension or swallowed by a massive UFO.

That said, the next target involves a UFO sighting and McMoneagle concurs in this case.

UFO Encounter

Target #3 was a sealed envelope with the following instructions on the outside:

1) Please Describe Target, 2) Describe Target's Origin, 3) Describe Target's Current Location.

Inside the envelope was a date and a brief description of my UFO encounter (described in Chapter 8) that took place one month after I flew through the heart of the Bermuda Triangle.

To clarify again, Joe did not know the nature of the target. However, if he remote viewed the targets in order, he would no doubt suspect that this target also related to the Bermuda Triangle. Regardless, his description of the target reaffirmed his uncanny talent to see targets at a distance not only in space, but in time.

Here's his description as he wrote it:

An elongated flat metallic pancake-shaped object with a highly polished surface showing no openings, traveling at a moderate speed of approximately 350 mph in a straight line at approximately 11,000 feet, at approximately 8:50 p.m. in a general north-northwestern direction, enveloped in a soft aura giving off a general whitish to blue-white wash with tinges of gold to reddish-gold around the edges that flash from time to time as though setting bits of air on fire. The object appears to wobble or vibrate to some extent and change course left to right—but this might be a change in perception or focus while watching the object, or be perceived as such. Observers of the object viewed it in close proximity for approximately ten to fifteen minutes after which it appeared to either wink out or speed off at tremendous speed.

Target's Origin: Basically unknown in that there is no way of formally identifying the specific place of origin. Mode of ingress/egress I believe to be intra-dimensional. Place of origin—elsewhere.

Current Location: Elsewhere. Will take some really difficult RV work and some degree of work re-defining how I describe reality to put it together. That will take considerable time. It might be doable, but I'm not sure yet how I would even begin to do it. Need to really sit down and think about it.

Joe also included a drawing of a pancake-shaped craft with an aura around its edges. He described the color of the vehicle as "whitish to blue-white with tinges of gold to reddish-gold around the edges." What I saw appeared to be glowing orange in tone and rather than flat like a pancake, there was a noticeable hump in the center on the topside.

There's an odd postscript on this one. After reading all this incredible information from Joe, it was difficult to believe he could do it without even seeing what was inside the envelope. But Rob insisted that was how he worked.

I got to spend time with Joe when I invited him and Rob down to my house in the Florida Keys to spend the night and go fishing with me first thing in the morning. I was interested in the behavior of a famous psychic. We had a great time together and caught a lot of bottom fish the next day; to my surprise, Joe seemed like a perfectly normal guy. But then just before he was leaving he did something unusual: He came up to me and appeared to be a little upset. He said to me "that UFO didn't have fins in the back of it like I had drawn, did it?" I told him no, but it was amazing to me that he even knew the target in the sealed envelope was a UFO. He said he couldn't understand why he had drawn the fins because he didn't think they were there, but he drew them anyway. I told him not to worry about it, but I could see he was still upset with himself.

It was about a year later when I was reviewing my files related to the Bermuda Triangle that I came upon the remote viewing documents. When I reached the target about the encounter with the UFO, I couldn't believe my eyes. The sketch of the UFO had no fins! I am absolutely positive he did *not* give me a revised copy of the sketch. Could it be possible that through his remote viewing capabilities he was able to revise the sketch without physically doing it? Maybe I have a mental block and forgot that he gave me a revised drawing. Whatever the case, I now believe he is one of the world's most capable remote viewers.

AUTEC

We were also interested in seeing what Joe would pick up on AUTEC, the Navy's base on Andros Island that we wrote about in Chapter 9. Would he see any kind of secret UFO research taking place there as some have suggested? Remote viewing government facilities was McMoneagle's bread and butter while working with Project Stargate. So we suspected this one would be an easy target for him. We were correct. When he completed the task in an hour and a half, he remarked: "This one was easier."

Inside the sealed envelope for Target #4 were two aerial photos of the AUTEC base. On the outside of the envelope, McMoneagle was asked:

Describe purpose of the target. 2) Is target related to target #1? If so, how?

The following is his written description of the remote viewing session, which was sent to us along with the reports on the other three targets:

Target is a collection of small single-level buildings of CBS construction, with what appear to be some sort of metal-like roofing or possibly white reflective type roofing for heat protection. The buildings are in neat rows or segments, and are much longer than they are wide. The scale of the buildings gives them the appearance of being elongated, like they may have entrances at each end—something like barracks buildings or buildings that are built for the purpose of ventilation or to encourage ventilation.

There is a mix of different types of buildings. There are approximately 60% of the elongated types of buildings, 20% trailer or temporary types of structures—which are predominately white and appear very bright in sunlight, and there are four or five larger and more permanent structures that appear to be some kind of operational buildings of some kind. These operational buildings are interconnected and circled with high fences of wire—what appears to be chain link fencing, which appears to be doubled in some places.

There is a cluster of four very large white buildings or possibly trailers that are encircled with double courses of chain link fencing, and these fences are topped with courses of barbed (concertina).

Off to one side there appears to be very large flat areas of concrete, some sort of catch basins or containment areas connected to large tanks (appears to be a row of three, possibly four tanks, all painted gray). The predominant colors on these buildings appears to be gray and white.

Entry to and from this facility also appears to be controlled with a formal gate which is constructed of concrete and guarded by people dressed in white—what appears to be white shorts and white shirts and carrying guns. Most other persons working within the facility are wearing blue, dark and light blue or tan working clothes. There are also some people wearing tropical sport shirts.

There are very few vehicles. What vehicles are visible are gray or light blue in color, and parked in what appears to be a motor pool area with white and yellow tanks behind a long low flat building toward the entry area. Also to the front of this building is an area of grass (what appears to be the only area of grass), and a set of three flag poles with flags flying from all three poles. I get a very strong sense that this is a mixed facility of both military as well as civilian personnel—about fifty/fifty.

On the opposite end from the entry road there is a very large flat area that has been leveled and flattened, which is approximately fifty acres and has been filled with what appears to be a crushed mixture of soft stone, clay, and calcium (maybe sea-shells or conch shells—smells like conch shells as they have a distinct smell when they have been crushed. I remember them from the Bahamas).

On this flat base area, there appears to be quite a display of wires strung in all different fashion of antennas. I say antennas, but many of these do not appear to be any I have ever sensed before. They are cut funny, as if they have been electronically buggered in some fashion, or otherwise "futzed" with. There is a very exotic ground-plane system and electronic frequency-tuning system involved here, as well as some sort of a sophisticated monitoring system emplaced which is in twenty-four hour operation. I'm also getting a very strong sensitivity feeling about the equipment that these antennas feed back into electronically—not sensitive in the sense of electronics, but sensitive in the sense of SECURITY. These systems are associated to special access programs and darkened projects, as well as high-level security systems attached to or having to do with submarine communications, tracking, and identifications. Less said from here on the better. Moving on . . .

To the south side of the antenna area there is a telemetry area, and up-link/down-link area that is tied directly to a small weather station and down range tracking system, which is also tied directly to the communications vans across the compound. I get a strong sensation that this in turn is tied directly into the down range tracking facilities in support of Cape Canaveral. I believe this is not a primary station, but a sub-station or back up relay station for down range weather information, and communications relay to Cape Canaveral (civilian-run and operated).

Conclusion. This is a downrange weather station and communications relay for Cape Canaveral co-located with a probable United States Naval Base, doing some sort of submarine communications relay, tracking, and identification. The location given the antenna field and stylization of buildings, vehicles, people, smells, air, layout, etc., would be Bahamas (80%), Turks and Caicos (50%), Virgin Island (30%), and Leeward Islands (15%).

Is target related to Target #1: I don't believe this target could be related in any way to target number one. The only possibility would be if the pilot accidentally flew through a high-energy transmission of the up-link telemetry beam during an extended transmission (in excess of 10 seconds.) However, if that had occurred, it would have cooked the instrumentation, the engines would have quit, and the aircraft would have crashed. It would have also cooked the pilot. The plane also would have had to be directly overhead—in which case no transmission would have taken place. They historically do not transmit when aircraft are overhead. These things are checked using radar prior to transmissions of any duration.

Joe McMoneagle again showed why he was known as the military and CIA's Remote Viewer #001. During his years as a psychic spy, he described secret Russian facilities, including one in 1979 that housed a top-secret Soviet "Typhoon" class submarine. In mid-January 1980, satellite photos confirmed his remote viewing of the hidden vessel.

While remote viewing such targets, he worked in the blind, not knowing what the target was, much less what he would find that was unknown to those who were seeking new information. So it wasn't surprising that McMoneagle's description of a Navy base in Andros Island was detailed and his description of the purpose of the base fit what is publically known about it. Although Joe found no UFOs hovering over the base or a direct connection to my flight in 1970, he did make reference to "special access programs and darkened projects." But he stopped short of looking any deeper into them.

Chapter 13

The Mystery Beyond

Probably more than any other living person, I've promoted the story of the Bermuda Triangle through appearances on cable channel documentaries, radio show interviews, our first book, *THE FOG*, and untold numbers of casual conversations with people I've met throughout the years. As anyone who know me knows, I'm not shy about talking about the Bermuda Triangle. I once even wrote the famed physicist Stephen Hawking about my experience, and he responded by sending me a copy of a lecture he gave in 1995 called "Space and Time Warps." (I quoted from that lecture at the end of Chapter 10.) I have made these efforts through the years primarily because my extraordinary experience defies all ordinary explanations. I know it happened; I lived it.

I've also discovered an elusive phenomenon: electronic fog. It has yet to be proven in a way that is acceptable to mainstream science. However, science couldn't explain the phenomenon of electricity until the late 18th century, even though various manifestations of electricity had been known since antiquity. Likewise, until 1802 scientists adamantly refused to believe that rocks occasionally fall from the sky. That was considered a superstition because meteorites were not part of the scientific paradigm of the time. Eventually, scientific proof was obtained and meteors and meteorites were accepted. No doubt some scientists, who had previously laughed at the idea of rocks falling from the sky, said they knew it all along.

Similar to many other questionable theories put forth in the past, I believe that one day electronic fog will be accepted as part of our environmental reality. However, I'm well aware that throughout the decades, skeptical researchers as well as scientific and military organizations have dismissed the Bermuda Triangle as a popular myth—a myth, that is, in the sense of being a misguided belief or fantasy.

In 1974, the same year that Charles Berlitz's *Bermuda Triangle* was published, the U.S. Navy released a brief report calling the Bermuda Triangle an imaginary area and cited bad weather as the likely culprit for the loss of ships and planes, including Flight 19. The statement remained unchanged for at least 30 years, and was readily available on the Navy's website. Then, in 2004, Gian Quasar's *Into the Bermuda Triangle* was published, followed in 2005 by our book, *THE FOG*. As if in response to our mention that the Navy still publicized its original statement with no updates, the report vanished.

Meanwhile, the U.S. Coast Guard stepped in with its own assessment in a similar vein as the Navy's deleted report. The Coast Guard does not recognize the existence of the "so-called Bermuda Triangle as a geographic area of specific hazard to ships or planes." The report says that the Coast Guard has reviewed many cases of lost aircraft and vessels through the years, and nothing was discovered that would indicate any "extraordinary factors" contributing to the losses. The Coast Guard also notes that the U.S. Board of Geographic Names doesn't recognize the Bermuda Triangle as an official name and doesn't maintain an official file on the area.

Surprisingly, the National Oceanic and Atmospheric Administration (NOAA) takes a broader perspective. Rather than a terse dismissal, NOAA provides a more congenial approach, describing the Bermuda Triangle "as a region in the western part of the

Atlantic Ocean in which ships, planes, and people are alleged to have mysteriously vanished." NOAA goes on to say that "the fabled Bermuda Triangle has captured the human imagination," and NOAA also recognizes that the Bermuda Triangle is a place where compasses don't always behave as expected and "disruptions in geomagnetic lines of flux" might exist there.

After giving a nod to the legend, the article points out that environmental factors, such as treacherous weather and shallow water near islands, probably account for many, if not most, disappearances. NOAA also explains: "There is no evidence that mysterious disappearances occur with any greater frequency in the Bermuda Triangle than in any other large, well-traveled area of the ocean."

Meanwhile, websites and blogs that focus on skepticism and debunking the paranormal tend to be far more hostile toward the Bermuda Triangle, dismissing it as a non-mystery. They attribute all the missing airplanes and ships to mechanical failures, human error, or bad weather, and reject any explanations that sound suspiciously supernatural.

Certainly, many disappearances were the result of severe storms, bad decisions, and ships that were unfit to set sail. Yet, to dismiss all that has occurred as a non-mystery is short-sighted. I wish a couple of hard-core, no-nonsense skeptics had been with me on my flight in 1970. I'm sure they wouldn't be so quick to dismiss the Bermuda Triangle.

That said, skeptics make a good point when they note that similar disappearances involving planes and ships have taken place outside the boundaries of the Bermuda Triangle. In fact, I now contend there is *no* Bermuda Triangle, but places throughout the world—inside and outside perceived triangles—where electronic fog can appear and even lead to space-time warps with baffling consequences.

Besides the Bermuda Triangle, disappearances seem to happen in other bodies of water, such as the Great Lakes, the seas off the Southeast coast of Japan to the Mariana Islands to the Philippines. I also include the South China Sea, the location of Malaysian Flight 370 when it disappeared from radar.

I believe there is a good possibility that the mysterious disappearance of the Malaysian Airlines flight on March 8, 2014, was linked to electronic fog. It's an explanation that literally flies below the radar of the mainstream media.

The first indication the airliner may have been in trouble was when the copilot signed off from Malaysian air traffic control. He said, "All right, good night." Normally, the pilot would say something like, "Malaysian 370 contacting Vietnam at 128.4. Thank you, goodnight."

Maybe the fog had just attached itself to the aircraft so the pilot cut the procedure short. The cockpit never contacted Vietnam airspace and strange things started occurring immediately after that last call.

Here is what I think might have happened:

The electronic fog disabled the radios, and all the readings on the Boeing 777's glass panel cockpit turned blank. The pilots had no idea of their exact heading because even the whisky compass was spinning. At that point, they were relying on mechanical backup instruments— the altimeter, the airspeed indicator, and the attitude indicator—to maintain control.

They turned about 120 degrees to the left, trying to aim for the nearest airport. They flew higher—to more than 43,000 feet—as they tried to get above the fog, then down to a few thousand feet in an attempt to fly under it. But the fog continued to cloak the aircraft.

They made more turns, hoping to lose the fog and find land and an airport. The pilots may have been able to maintain their autopilot, but the heading would have to be controlled by their input. After going through a series of turns, they became disoriented and, like Flight 19, they continued until they ran out of fuel. Also, like Flight 19, they disappeared in a remote location of ocean where they may never be found.

With no recognition of electronic fog by mainstream science, my scenario is not even being considered as a possible solution to the mystery of the Malaysian airliner. It's a rare phenomenon, but I know it's real not only because I have experienced it, but so have other pilots.

Clearing the Fog

Meteorologists recognize the existence of magnetic anomalies in certain places in the world, including the Atlantic Ocean off the coast of Florida. They also acknowledge that static electricity from electromagnetic storms can knock out electronic instruments in airplanes. However, at present, electronic fog is a mere rumor.

Scientists say that fog doesn't "stick" to airplanes and electromagnetic storms don't create warp bubbles or breach the space-time continuum. However, I believe that eventually electronic fog will shift from anomalous experience to scientific fact in the same way that we now recognize electricity and meteorites. David Pares, a former army meteorologist and physics professor, provided a sound scientific logic for the existence of electronic fog in his analysis of my flight in Chapter 11. I also think that space-time distortions related to electronic fog and electromagnetic energy fields may become a fact in the same sense that we have harnessed electricity.

Just imagine the awesome powers we would possess if we could instantaneously travel between planets or move through time. In that world, it wouldn't take a lifetime to reach the nearest planet compatible with our own.

Similar to atomic energy, the power to leap worlds or enter the future or past could be used for good or evil purposes depending on who was making the decisions. Maybe the reason that scientists haven't recognized electronic fog and its link to breaches in the space-time continuum is because we're not ready for it yet. Maybe it will remain in the realm of science fiction until the human race evolves far enough to deal with the awesome powers that would result from the ability to open doors at will to what lies beyond.

I want to finish with a few "modest" predictions that were inspired by the writings of Arthur C. Clarke.

- By the year 2030 there will be the first official contact with extra-terrestrial life.
- By the year 2050, electronic fog will be harnessed, and a space warp drive will be a reality.
- By the year 2060, advances in quantum gravity research will open pathways to time travel.
- By 2070 there will be near-light speeds and interstellar flight.
- By the year 2100 we will be meeting with space aliens. If we go to war against them, we lose. If we avoid war, we will travel with them throughout the Milky Way.

Finally, a quote from Clarke, who ended episodes of his TV series, *Mysterious World,* (on which I appeared), by saying: "The universe not only seems stranger than we can imagine, it is stranger that we can imagine, and the only way to discover the limits of the possible is to go beyond them into the impossible."

BIBLIOGRAPHY

Berlitz, Charles. *Bermuda Triangle: The Greatest Unsolved Mystery of Our Time.* New York: Doubleday, 1974.

———. *The Dragon's Triangle.* London: Grafton Books, 1990.

———. *Planes That Never Landed.*

———. *Without a Trace.* New York: Ballantine Books, 1977.

Bierend, Doug. "That Physicist in Omaha is Still Working on a Warp Drive in his Garage." *Motherboard,* July 20, 2015, *https://motherboard.vice.com /en_us/article/that-physicist-in-omaha-is-still-working-on-a-warp-drive -in-his-garage*

Billings, Lee. "Time Travel Simulation Resolves 'Grandfather Paradox." *Scientific American,* 2 September, 2014. *www.scientificamerican.com /article/time-travel-simulation-resolves-grandfather-paradox/*

Caidin, Martin. *Ghosts of the Air: True Stories of Aerial Hauntings.* Lakeville, Minn.: Galde Press, 1994.

Dolan, Richard. *UFOs and the National Security State.* Rochester, N.Y.: Keyhole Publishing, 2009.

Drake, Rufus. "The Deadly Mystery of Japan's Bermuda Triangle." *Saga,* April 1976.

"Fear U.S. Tanker Sinks Near Japan," Chicago Tribune, Nov. 27, 1967.

Friday, David M., Broughton, Peter B., et al. "Further Insight into the Nature of Ball-Lightening-Like Atmospheric Pressure Plasmoids." *The Journal of Physical Chemistry,* 117, 39 (2013): 9931–9940.

Good, Timothy. *Unearthly Disclosure.* London: Century Random House, 2000.

Goddard, Victor. *Flight Towards Reality.* London: Turnstone Books, 1975.

Hawking, Stephen. *Space and Time Warps.* Lecture. October 18, 1995.

History Channel. *UFO Files,* "The Pacific Bermuda Triangle," *www .mercuryrapids.co.uk/articles/UFOFilesPacificBermudaTriangle.htm*

Kusche, Larry. *The Bermuda Triangle Mystery Solved.* Amherst, N.Y.: Prometheus Books, 1995.

————. *The Disappearance of Flight 19.* New York: Harper & Row, 1980.

Lindbergh, Charles. *Autobiography of Values.* San Diego: Harcourt Brace Jovanovich, 1978.

MacGregor, Rob, and Bruce Gernon. *THE FOG: A Never Before Published Theory of the Bermuda Triangle Phenomenon.* St. Paul, Minn.: Llewellyn Books, 2005.

Maroco, Andy. *Flight 19 Complete Naval Report: Testimony & Exhibits (Volumes 1 & 2).* Blurb Books, 2016.

Mills, Marc. "Is Warp Drive Real," NASA website, March 10, 2015.

Mori, Masaru. "The female alien in a hollow vessel." *Fortean Times* 48 (1987): 48–50.

Pares, David. *Science Behind Bruce Gernon's Flight 4 December 1970. www .stealthskater.com/Documents/Bermuda_02.pdf*

Preisinger, Dr. Michael. *Das Bermuda-Rätsel gelöst.* Munich: Langen Muller, 1997.

Quasar, Gian J. *Into the Bermuda Triangle: Pursuing the Truth Behind the World's Greatest Mystery.* New York: McGraw-Hill, 2004.

Ringbauer, Martin, and Matthew A. Broome, et al. "Experimental Simulation of Closed Timelike Curves." *Nature Communications,* online article number: 4145 (2014), June 19, 2014. *www.nature.com/articles /ncomms5145*

Rose, Kenneth. *King George V.* New Haven, Conn.: Phoenix Press, 2000.

Tanaka, Kazuo. "Did a close encounter of the Third Kind occur on a Japanese beach in 1803?" *Skeptical Inquirer* 24, 4 (2000): 37–60.

Trantham, Cary. "Surviving Get-Home-Itis." *AOPA Pilot,* April 2003.

Travel Channel. *World of Mysteries: Bermuda Triangle: Lost at Sea.* 2002.

Tune, Ray Loyd. *It's Only a Delusion if it Doesn't Work: Everyone Has a Delusion—What's Yours?* Bloomington, Ill.: Xlibris, 2014.

VanNatta, Jr., Don. "Bermuda Triangles Deep Secret Preserved 5 Sunken Planes Aren't Lost Patrol." *Miami Herald,* June 5, 1991.

UFO Sightings UFO Files: The Pacific Bermuda Triangle. 4avi New Videos. *www.youtube.com/watch?v=NbiqvInMTlI*

Wagner, Richard. *The Legend of the Flying Dutchman. www.musicwith ease.com*

Walia, Arjun. "Physicists Send Particles of Light into the Past, Proving Time Travel is Possible?" *Collective Evolution,* 7 December, 2015. *www.collective-evolution.com/2015/12/07/physicists-send-particles-of-light -into-the-past-proving-time-travel-is-possible/*

INDEX

ABOUT THE AUTHORS

Bruce Gernon is a certified seaplane flight instructor and a master captain with a Coast Guard license. A real estate broker, commercial building contractor, and owner of Keys Properties, Bruce has appeared in 36 cable channel documentaries about the Bermuda Triangle in which he describes his space-time–warp experience, often as the featured interview. He also coined the term "electronic fog." Bruce resides in Boynton Beach, Florida, with his wife, Lynn.

Rob MacGregor coauthored *THE FOG* with Bruce Gernon and has published 20 novels and 24 non-fiction books. An author of seven Indiana Jones novels, he has been on the *New York Times* best-seller list and is a winner of the Edgar Allan Poe Award for mystery writing for his novel *Prophecy Rock*. His most recent non-fiction title is *Sensing the Future: A Field Guide to Precognition*, coauthored with his wife, Trish (T.J.) MacGregor. The MacGregors reside in Wellington, Florida.